LEARNING BABYLON.JS

Written by Julian Chenard

@temechon

temechon@gmail.com

Cover by Jean-Baptiste Bledowski

@jbledowski

This book is sold at http://learningbabylonjs.com

This version was originally published in September 2015, **and updated in March 2017**.

Please do not distribute or share this book without permission.

ABOUT ME

Hi! My name is Julian Chenard, I'm a French 30 years-old engineer currently working as WebGL developer in Rouen (not so far from Paris if you were wondering). I create 3D applications during the day and 3D games and experiences at night using Babylon.js.

I created these small games/experiences with this framework (and few others), all available at http://www.pixelcodr.com :

- <u>Shinobomb</u>, a remake of the Bomberman classic
- <u>Block</u>, a puzzle-game
- <u>Quarto</u>, a remake of the eponym board game
- <u>Christmas Runner</u>, an infinite runner
- <u>Kicker</u>, a free kick arcade game
- <u>Procedural-city</u>, the automatic creation of a random city

I'm also one of Babylon.js admin team on Github, and a contributor for almost 4 years of this engine. I created a plugin to plug Babylon.js to the physics engine Oimo.js (used now as the default physics engine of Babylon.js, recently reworked by my friend Raanan), took part in the creation of the official Babylon.js documentation, and added a way to read OBJ files directly from Babylon.js. Recently I worked on the new debug layer (you will see later in this book), that replaced the old ugly version.

3

Two years ago, I created several free tutorials to get started with Babylon.js on my website. I also give some training courses about Babylon.js (alongside my full-time job) at Isart Digital, a video game and 3D animation school in Paris, and in a French public establishment (IUT MMI Elbeuf)

This book was for me the opportunity to combine two things I like doing: create WebGL games and share my passions with others.

TABLE OF CONTENTS

Table of contents

Table of contents

PREFACE

I'm creating 3D engines since I was 16. The first one was written with pure C for DOS and then I followed the technology with various versions for 3DFX, DirectX or XNA.

All the learning that I gathered during 24 years of coding was applied to create Babylon.js. The project started in 2013 with my old friend David Rousset when we decided to create a 3D engine for web developers with one goal in mind: simplicity. We wanted to allow any JavaScript developer to unleash all the raw power of their GPU without having to deal with maths, shaders and all the weird creatures that live in this world.

We now have a strong community who helps us adding new features and teaching how to use all the wonders that lie inside Babylon.js. But I sincerely have to admit that I'm extremely proud that Julian wrote this book. Can you imagine that? Someone who writes a book (And thus dedicates a lot of personal time) about one of your project! For me this is the best gift I could receive.

But I'm also impressed by the quality of this book. Julian completely understood the foundation of Babylon.js. He wrote his book with the same goal:

Let's keep things simple!

David Catuhe, *creator of Babylon.js*

Book organisation

This book is divided into 14 chapters.

Chapter 1, Hello World in 3D talks about the steps to have a cube displayed in the browser using Babylon.js.

Chapter 2, Discover basic elements covers the basic elements that can be used in Babylon.js: mesh, camera and lights.

Chapter 3, Design and debug your game focus on some useful concepts to help the developer (you!) to create your game.

Chapter 4 Working with classes explains how to create game entities and use them in your game.

Chapter 5, Materials shows how to create, apply and update materials to your game entities.

Chapter 6, Exporters talks about some exporters to create a Babylon file.

Chapter 7, Reading and using a Babylon file describes how to read and use a Babylon file in your game.

Chapter 8, Animations, shows how you can create and set animations for your objects.

Chapter 9, User inputs introduces how to move the player in your virtual world with a keyboard or a gamepad.

Chapter 10, Using a physics engine describes how to use an external physics engine called Oimo.js to add some physics properties to your game.

Chapter 11, Collisions and actions talks about how to use two different systems to handle collisions between your game objects.

Chapter 12, Skeletons and Bones system adds an animated character into the game.

Chapter 13, Eyes candies, talks about particles and shaders to make your game look shiny and beautiful.

Chapter 14, Improving performance, shows the use of some concepts to improve the performance of your application.

How this book works

The purpose of this book is to explain the creation of a complete little game. For each chapter, you will first see a small part of theory related to a concept of Babylon.js, then you will put it in practice at the end of the chapter.

How to draw an owl

1. Draw some circles   2. Draw the rest of the fucking owl

Figure 1 - How to draw an owl

In my opinion, the above image is a common problem in many books or tutorials: I will try not to make the same mistake by explaining everything you need to know to understand every addressed feature.

At the end of some chapters, a cheat sheet will sum up all important points.

Who this book is for

This book is intended for developers interested in 3D game development for the web, or already familiar with WebGL and wanting to discover the world of Babylon.js. No prior knowledge of Babylon.js is needed, but basic understanding of JavaScript, HTML and CSS is assumed.

The tools you need

Browser support

It is important to know that WebGL (and thus Babylon.js) is not supported by all browsers. However, it is very easy to fulfil this requirement by downloading a newer version of your browser (or completely switching to a different browser if necessary). If you don't know whether your browser supports WebGL or not, try to access to the following website: https://get.webgl.org/

If you can see a spinning cube, the answer is yes. Otherwise, a message should appear saying your browser is not up to date. You can then click on the suggested link to upgrade your browser.

Here are the minimal versions of browsers supporting Babylon.js:

- Internet Explorer 11: Microsoft is late to the WebGL party, but the last version of its browser now supports it rather well. WebGL support will be much better in the next browser to come: Microsoft Edge.
- Microsoft Edge: The latest browser of MS, shipped with Windows 10, supports extremely well WebGL.
- Firefox 4+: version 41 is recommended.
- Chrome 9+ version 43 is recommended.
- Safari 5.1: version 8 is recommended.
- Opera 12+: Even with the latest version, the support is not optimal.

Basically, Babylon.js runs on the latest version of all modern browsers.

On mobile, all browsers are now supporting WebGL (except Opera Mini which does not support WebGL at all), but the experience should be created specifically for mobile platforms in order to optimize the game accordingly.

Software

As Babylon.js is a Javascript framework, all you need to start is a text editor and a supported browser. If you work with external assets (textures, videos, 3D models...) you will need a local server.

I recommend the following text editors:

- **WebStorm** (Paid): WebStorm is a powerful IDE made by JetBRAINS, perfectly equipped for JavaScript applications. It is cross-platform, has JavaScript and TypeScript support (with full autocompletion), built-in watchers and compilers, Github/SVN integration, Node.js support... I cannot think of something that WebStorm doesn't have. It is my IDE of choice.

- **Visual Studio** (Paid and Free): Visual Studio is also a very powerful IDE made by Microsoft. It supports a lot of programming language such as JavaScript and TypeScript, but also C, C#, Python... You will find in VS at least as many features as in WebStorm.
- **Visual Studio Code** (Free): Recently announced by Microsoft in 2015, this editor is based on Github's Atom editor. It is lightweight, cross-platform, has Intellisense support, Github integration, and JavaScript/TypeScript support. Very powerful and very interesting.
- **Atom** (Free): The editor created by Github. Very interesting as it is completely modular.

If you use WebStorm or Visual Studio, you can use their integrated local server:

- WebStorm: http://localhost:63342/**project**/index.html
- Visual Studio: http://localhost:9606/index.html

If you don't, you will have to use a local web server. I recommend using WAMP (http://www.wampserver.com/) as it is very easy to use.

Reader feedback

I would love to hear your feedback about this book. Let me know what you liked or disliked by sending me an email at julian.chenard@gmail.com, I'll be happy to answer you ☺

INTRODUCTION

Nowadays, you can find and play more games on the web than on any other platform: PC, consoles, tablets, mobiles. You can play MMO games, such as Dofus or Runescape. You can play Flappy Bird clones, Tetris clones, Farmville clones. And I can't count the number of web-games released for the Ludum Dare game jam (more than 1500 different games for LD32!).

Never more than today has the modern web become a viable platform not only to promote your game, but also for creating stunning, high quality games: kick-ass 3D MMORPGs, action games, shooters, adventure, and more. All this with no more than a web browser (and maybe a gamepad, but we will talk about it later).

Babylon.js is a way of building such 3D games. If your dream game is a 3D multiplayer shooter Flappy Bird-like (note to self: I may have an idea here), or an animated/scripted fan-fiction of Geralt from the Witcher universe, you CAN create and build it with Babylon.js.

Figure 2 - Screenshot from the game Assassin's Creed Race

What is Babylon.js?

Let's first talk about the Web Graphics Library (**WebGL**). WebGL is a Javascript API used for rendering interactive 2D and 3D graphics within any compatible web browser: that means it is natively integrated into the browser, without any plugins (sorry Flash!). With WebGL, you can make use of the client computer GPU to render high-performance 3D computer graphics. However, the main drawback of this API is its complexity: programming WebGL directly from Javascript is a complex process that can be drastically eased by dedicated frameworks built above WebGL. There are several frameworks for this, and in this book we will focus on Babylon.js.

Babylon.js can be understood as a tool to give developers an abstract foundation to encapsulate complexes tasks with **simple** commands. Want to draw a cube? Just call the method CreateBox(). Same goes with Sphere, Cylinder, Torus, and so on. Want to set a color? Just write myCube.material.diffuseColor = red.

And the list goes on!

Figure 3 - Screenshot from the game Flight Arcade

Babylon.js is a JavaScript 3D engine built above WebGL, created by 3 awesome guys:

- David Catuhe, lead developer, also known as Deltakosh
- David Rousset, developer, also known as davrous
- Michel Rousseau, 3D artist

As this engine is fully open source (MIT-licensed, via Github - https://github.com/BabylonJS/Babylon.js), several other contributors can be added to this list (several dozen to date).

Babylon.js is built in TypeScript, a compiled language producing JavaScript. It gives several advantages:

- As it's a typed language, reading and understand TypeScript is easy because functions and parameters are typed.
- Static compilation
- Lambda expressions
- Real class inheritance

TypeScript is a super-set of Javascript, and is much better to develop a large-scaled application. It resolves a lot of problems introduced in Javascript (don't ever write var that = this again!), and it is strong-typed: you can benefit from the static compilation and it can help a lot to find bugs.

That doesn't mean you have to learn and use TypeScript! Keep in mind Babylon.js is a JavaScript library: only its source code is written in TypeScript. If you want to contribute to the framework, you will have to do it in TypeScript, and not in JavaScript.

What are we going to do?

In this book, we will learn to use Babylon.js by re-adapting an awesome game with very specific 3D features:

Figure 4 - Cover of Super Monkey Ball on GameCube

You may have recognized the game **Super Monkey Ball**, a game released in 2001 on arcade machines, and later on GameCube.

 Super Monkey Ball was developed by Amusement Vision. Two years later, Amusement Vision developed F-ZERO, an awesome racing video game.

Super Monkey Ball is a platform game where the player cannot move directly the character itself, but instead has to tilt the world to make the character move. By tilting the board at specific angles, the player can control the character's speed and direction.

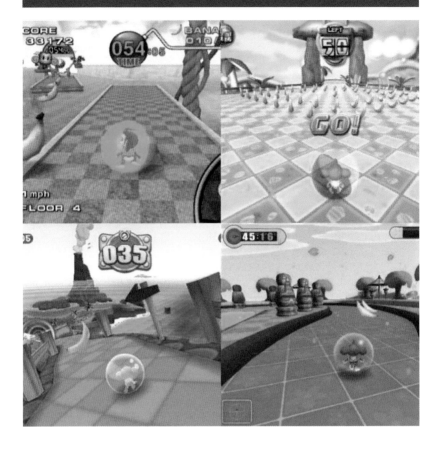

Figure 5 - Screenshot of several Super Monkey Ball games

The goal of each level is to get to the finish gate without falling off before the given time. The player can earn bonus points by collecting bananas.

The game we are going to create together will be very similar to Super Monkey Ball: the player is represented by a sphere, and the goal is to get to the finish gate without falling off the level. The difference from Super Monkey Ball is that the player will directly move the ball (and not the board). We will use this as a pretext to introduce how to use a basic physics engine with Babylon.js.

Along the way, some spikes will prevent the player from moving on: he will have to get the corresponding key to deactivate them.

The player has a limited number of lives for each level, and on top of that a timer is counting down to put more pressure on the player.

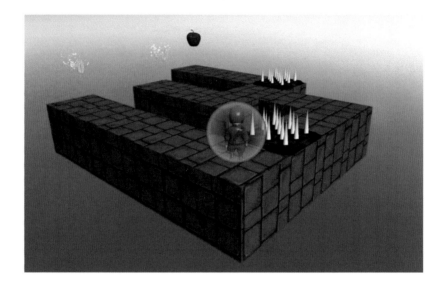

Figure 6 - A screenshot of the game you will make with this book's help

This game is simple, but complex enough to show many concepts of Babylon.js: simple 3D shapes, lights, colors, animations, collisions, actions, particles, physics, and more! It may seem difficult at first sight, but don't worry, everything you need to know will be detailed and explained. For some chapters, some exercises will make you experiment with the current concept in more detail.

We will build the game mechanics using only Javascript. This language is very well suited to create small games like this one, but you might be interested in moving to TypeScript if you want to build a larger game.

I strongly believe that learning to code is hard work. It requires much more than only knowing the theory. You must practice it yourself, watch others practicing, and practice again. I could teach you how to surf, teach you all the physics and the mathematics behind it, and you still would fall in the water the first time. Learning how to use a new framework is no different.

I strongly encourage you to code your own game while reading this book. Tweak all parameters, change the game level, or make the ball bounce when the player is moving it... Try new things! The whole concept of this book is to **learn by doing**.

Now that you know a little bit more about of the game we will create, we can break it down into several parts. Specifically, we will need to do the following:

Create the level

A level should be easily created by the developer (in order to reproduce it a lot), and displayed on screen.

Create the player

The player (the ball) is a specific entity that can be moved by the user: keyboard events should be hooked and handled by our game.

Use materials

Materials are used to color and texture our scene. We will learn how to use it.

Display custom 3D models

A game is much better looking with custom 3D models created by a professional. We will learn how to include such models.

Integrate a physics engine

The physics engine will make the player move... and fall.

Handle collisions

We need collisions in order to have the player collecting bonuses (and die with traps!).

Load an animated model

Our player will be a beautiful ninja animated with a skeleton!

Use eye candies

Particles and post processes are used to make your game shiny and beautiful.

Improve performance

Some concepts can be applied to improve the render time of your game.

We will start by creating a Babylon scene with basics elements: a sphere representing the player, boxes for the level, torus for keys, and so on. We will also decide on a data model to create our entities (or nodes as we will call it later) ...

In the next chapters, animations, materials, user inputs, and collisions will also be detailed, as well as every important notion to create a game like Super Monkey Ball.

Are you ready? Because I am :) Let's get started!

CHAPTER 1 - HELLO WORLD IN 3D

In this chapter, we will learn how to create the "hello world" program of Babylon.js: the minimum code to get a 3D cube rendering in the browser.

The HTML skeleton

Open your favorite text editor/IDE and copy-paste the snippet below. Save it in a new file called index.html.

```html
<!DOCTYPE html>
<html lang="en">
<head>
  <meta charset="UTF-8"/>
  <title>Hello World in Babylon.js</title>
  <script src="http://cdn.babylonjs.com/2-5/babylon.js"></script>
  <script src="helloWorld.js"></script>
  <style>
    html, body {
      margin   : 0;
      padding  : 0;
      overflow : hidden;
      width    : 100%;
      height   : 100%;
    }
    #gameCanvas {
      width    : 100%;
      height   : 100%;
    }
```

```
  </style>
</head>
<body>
  <canvas id="gameCanvas"></canvas>
</body>
</html>
```

The HTML part is really simple. You can see the Babylon library is included at the beginning of the page from the official CDN server. The small CSS part is used to remove the default HTML page margin. There are two things important here. The first is the use of the canvas element in the HTML body: it is this element that will be used to render all 3D elements in the page.

The second important thing is the use of an external script helloWorld.js in the head tag. This file contains all the magic: the 3D scene creation. No more suspense, here is the Javascript part.

Instead of using babylon.js from a CDN server, we could have downloaded it from the official repository and include the local copy in this project.

Several versions of the same library

In the introduction, we said that Babylon.js was an open-source project. Its source code is located on Github (https://github.com/BabylonJS/Babylon.js). By opening this URL in your browser, you will see the official repository:

The folder **src** contains all source files composing the framework. Don't hesitate to take a look at it to know how some features work internally.

The folder **dist** contains several files representing the whole framework:

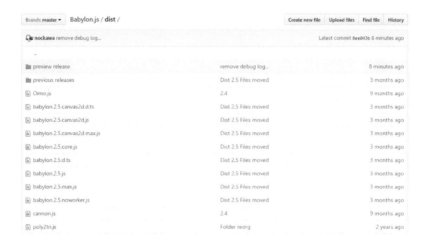

There are currently three versions of Babylon.js:

  - **babylon.2.5.noworker.js**, a version of Babylon that is built without web workers.

  - **babylon.2.5.js**, the minified version which is half the size of the debug version. You should use this version in production mode.

  - **babylon.2.5.max.js**, the debug version of the library which makes debugging much easier. You should use this version when you're working on your game.

All other files (Oimo.js, cannon.js and poly2tri.js) are dependencies for specific features of Babylon.js.

You can of course download the full repository and use the version you want (by default, there is no difference between the 3 versions.). In the next part, we will detail the JavaScript part of our first example. Don't forget to use the JavaScript console of your browser (F12 in most browsers to open the developer menu) to check if any Javascript error prevents you from seeing the 3D scene.

The JavaScript part

```
window.addEventListener("DOMContentLoaded", function() {

    // BABYLON Engine creation
    var canvas = document.getElementById('gameCanvas');
    var engine = new BABYLON.Engine(canvas, true);

    // BABYLON Scene creation
    var scene  = new BABYLON.Scene(engine);

    // The camera, necessary see the world
    var camera = new BABYLON.FreeCamera("camera", new BABYLON.Vector3(5,5,-
    5), scene);
    camera.setTarget(BABYLON.Vector3.Zero());

    // The ambient light
    var light  = new BABYLON.HemisphericLight("light", new BABYLON.Vector3(0,1,0),
    scene);

    // The cube
    var cube   = BABYLON.Mesh.CreateBox("myBox", 1, scene);

    // The render loop
    engine.runRenderLoop(function() {
       scene.render();
    });

}, false);
```

Wow, so many new things! Let's explain all of this step by step.

As I said earlier, the canvas element is mandatory in order to draw a 3D scene, and the developer must ensure it has been loaded by the browser. When the DOM is completely loaded, the browser sends the DOMContentLoaded event. This line simply retrieves it and links the 3D scene creation to it.

The following error is displayed in the console if you forget to hook the DOMContentLoaded event:

Uncaught TypeError: Cannot read property 'getBoundingClientRect' of null.

It means the canvas element is not fully loaded.

```
// BABYLON Engine creation
var canvas = document.getElementById('gameCanvas');
var engine = new BABYLON.Engine(canvas, true);
```

Here, the canvas element (which id is gameCanvas) is used to create a BABYLON.Engine. The engine is the object interacting with the low-level WebGL API. It's this object that will render the scene in the page. The first parameter to its constructor is the canvas DOM object, the second one is to enable anti-aliasing (false by default).

```
// BABYLON Scene creation
var scene = new BABYLON.Scene(engine);
```

The Babylon scene is created by passing the engine to its constructor. The scene is a container that stores all objects you need to render.

```
// The camera, necessary see the world
var camera = new BABYLON.FreeCamera("camera", new BABYLON.Vector3(5,5,-5), scene);
camera.setTarget(BABYLON.Vector3.Zero());
```

At least one camera is needed to display your scene. The first parameter is the object name, the second is the camera position, and the last one is the scene we created above. By default, a camera looks right in front of it (along the Z axis), but we want it to look at the scene's origin: the method camera.setTarget is used.

```
// The ambient light
var light = new BABYLON.HemisphericLight("light", new BABYLON.Vector3(0,1,0), scene);
```

An ambient light is created, well, to actually see something. For this, a Hemispheric light is used, because it simulates sun-light (casts light on everything in the scene along its direction – here {0, 1, 0}).

```
// The cube
var cube  = BABYLON.Mesh.CreateBox("myBox", 1, scene);
```

And here is the star of this first example: the cube! The first parameter is its name, the second is its size, and the last one is the Babylon scene.

If you try to run the project at this point, you won't probably see anything. That's because of the last step: the engine render loop.

```
// The render loop
engine.runRenderLoop(function() {
  scene.render();
});
```

The render loop is the main game loop: the loop that will render your scene (among other things, but we'll talk about it later). What it does is basically rendering the scene 60 times per second, (in order to get 60 frames per second, or FPS). If your scene contains a lot of heavy 3D models, a lot of textures or both, the frame will take more time to render, and it won't be possible for the engine to do it 60 times in a second: your FPS will drop, and the user will experience latency and lag. Under 30 FPS, your game/project will not be usable.

You can add to this function everything you need to be checked several times per second (user inputs, collisions, physics...), but we will see later in the next chapter a better way to do this.

Result

And here is the result! Awesome, isn't it?

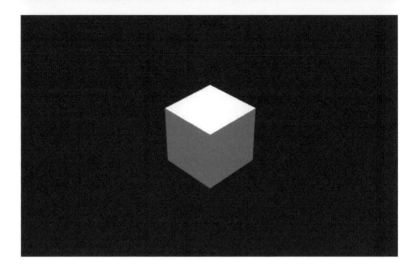

Figure 7 - "Hello World!" in Babylon.js

Now, before moving to the first real scene (the Super Monkey Ball game scene), some theoretical points will be addressed. These points will greatly help you in building your game scene and better understanding how the engine works internally.

Some things to know about Babylon.js

All 3D objects are called 'nodes'

And that is because Babylon.js is a complete scene graph. A scene graph is a data structure commonly used by 3D graphic editing applications and video games, which sorts from a logical point of view the spatial representation of a scene (generally a collection of nodes in a graph or tree structure). In Babylon, this means every scene can be represented as a tree, where the tree root is the scene, and each leaf can be a mesh, a material, a light or a camera. Everything added in the scene graph will be displayed (or at least 'used' to display something).

Why use a scene graph you might ask? Because this structure helps a lot for optimization. For example, it is really easy to group related meshes into a compound object that can be transformed as a single object. Another example would be instances: the logical object is kept in memory only once, but the graphical representation is displayed several times.

All nodes take a name in their constructor

And that is the case for mesh, material, light and camera. This way, you can retrieve an object by its name (very useful when working with 3D artists!) with the following methods:

```
scene.getMeshByName("myBox");
scene.getCameraByName("camera");
scene.getLightByName("light");
scene.getMaterialByName("material");
```

However, this name is not mandatory, and you can set it to an empty string if you don't use it. Similarly, you can have several objects with the same name: that's why all these methods will return the last object added to the scene.

Even if it's not mandatory, try to always use a representative name, as it will greatly help you in your debug phase.

Babylon uses a left-handed coordinate systems

It is important to note the spatial coordinate system used by Babylon is a 'left-handed y-up system'. That means the z-axis points forward, the y-axis points up, and the x-axis points right. The positive rotation is clockwise about the axis of rotation.

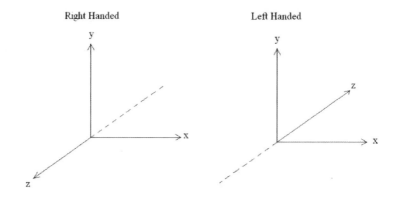

Figure 8 - Right-handed and left-handed coordinate systems

With your left hand, if you place your thumb along the x-axis and the index finger along the y-axis, the middle finger will be aligned with the z-axis. You won't be able to do the same with a right-handed system (unless you're trying with your right hand of course).

This system is just a convention that may be different for other engines. You should keep it in mind when designing scenes in Babylon (to set up cameras for example).

World space and local space

When we want to render a 3D scene, the first step is to put all models in the same space, the world space. The origin of the world space is the point (0, 0, 0), and in this world space, all objects have a position. In the picture below, the cube is at the position (1, 1, 1).

Within this world space, we can give to each object a position, a rotation, and a scale. All these transformations describes a local space. We will talk about it again later, don't worry. Just remember the world space is the same for all objects, and the local space is specific to a given object.

In Babylon.js (and in other 3D engines), a local space is called a **world matrix**.

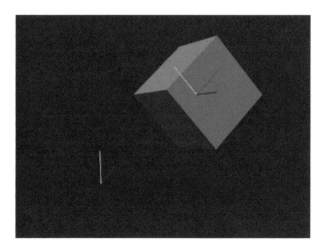

Figure 9 - World space and local space

Exercise

Create a scene with the following elements:

-   a hemispheric light lighting the scene from below
-   a camera located in (0, 5, −15) and looking at the point (0,0,0)
-   6 cubes along the x axis.

Your final scene should look like the following picture:

CHEAT SHEET

HTML part

```
<canvas id="gameCanvas"></canvas>
```

Create an engine

```
var canvas = document.getElementById('gameCanvas');
var engine = new BABYLON.Engine(canvas, true);
```

Create a scene

```
var scene  = new BABYLON.Scene(engine);
```

Create a basic camera

```
var camera = new BABYLON.FreeCamera(name, position, scene);
```

Create a basic light

```
var light  = new BABYLON.HemisphericLight(name, direction, scene);
```

Set the render loop

```
engine.runRenderLoop(function() {
 scene.render();
});
```

Get a mesh by name (same with cameras, lights and materials)

```
var mesh = scene.getMeshByName(name);
```

Babylon is a left-handed Y-up coordinates system

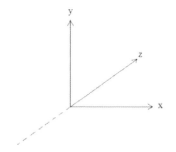

CHAPTER 2 - DISCOVER BASIC ELEMENTS

In this chapter, we will describe the basic elements of Babylon.js: meshes, cameras and lights.

This chapter is not supposed to be exhaustive, as describing all the available features is not the main concept of this book. However, some common objects are detailed.

Don't worry, we get back to practice in the next chapter!

Babylon.js basic elements

Scene

A scene is one of the first objects you need to use in order to display something in your browser, and one of the most important. Indeed, this object will contain all 3D objects (meshes, lights, cameras...) and all materials needed to render your game. If this object is empty, nothing will be shown!

A game can have several scenes, each of these corresponding to a different environment: a scene with the world map, a scene with the inside of a building, and so on.

Moreover, the scene object provides several ways to control your game environment: updating the ambient light color, adding fog... Understanding and controlling this object is the first step to creating beautiful games ☺

This object provides several interesting attributes and methods described here. Keep in mind this list is far from exhaustive: you can read the official documentation for this.

Scene attributes

clearColor	Takes a BABYLON.Color4, and represents the scene's background color.
ambientColor	Same as above, but represents the scene's ambient color.
fogEnabled	True if the fog should be enabled, false otherwise (false by default).
lights	Contains all lights from the scene
meshes	Contains all meshes from the scene
cameras	Contains all cameras from the scene
materials	Contains all materials from the scene
multiMaterials	Contains all multi-materials from the scene
textures	Contains all textures from the scene
particleSystems	Contains all particle systems from the scene
skeletons	Contains all skeletons from the scene
activeCamera	Represents the currently active camera
activeCameras	Contains all active cameras (in case of multiple point of views). All these cameras are active at the same time.
debugLayer	The scene debug layer. See chapter 3 for more info.

The highlighted attributes are very useful if you want to iterate over a complete collection of items. For example, if you want to disable all lights, or disable all textures.

Scene methods

getEngine()	Returns the Babylon engine of the game
getTotalVertices()	Returns the total number of vertices of the scene
getActiveMeshes()	Returns an instance of an array containing all visible meshes from the scene
registerBeforeRender()	Takes a function as a parameter. This function will be called just before rendering the scene (60 times per second if possible).
registerAfterRender()	Same as above, but the function is called after rendering.
unregisterBeforeRender()	Remove a function added with the previous method
unregisterAfterRender()	Same as above
executeWhenReady()	Takes a function as a parameter, and execute this function when the scene is ready to be displayed (all meshes and materials are ready)
render()	Render the scene to the screen. Should be used in the engine render loop (as seen in 0)
pick()	Create and launch a ray in order to select a mesh with the mouse pointer. Takes two screen coordinates as a parameter.

Meshes

There are currently 9 basic elements in Babylon.js (from version 2.1), and the framework has a dedicated static method to build each of these primitives, as described in the following table:

Box	BABYLON.Mesh.CreateBox(name, size, scene)
Sphere	BABYLON.Mesh.CreateSphere(name, segments, diameter, scene)
Plane	BABYLON.Mesh.CreatePlane(name, size, scene)
Cylinder	BABYLON.Mesh.CreateCylinder(name, height, diameterTop, diameterBot, tessellation, subdivision, scene)

Torus	BABYLON.Mesh.CreateTorus(name, diameter, thickness, tessellation, scene);
Torus Knot	BABYLON.Mesh.CreateTorusKnot(name, radius, tube, radialSegments, tubularSegments, p, q, scene)
Line	BABYLON.Mesh.CreateLines(name, points, scene)
Ribbon	BABYLON.Mesh.CreateRibbon(name, path, closeArray, closePath, offset, scene)
Tube	BABYLON.Mesh.CreateTube(name, path, radius, tessellation, radiusFunction, cap, scene)

All these methods are perfectly described in the official documentation here: http://doc.babylonjs.com/tutorials/discover_basic_elements, and I strongly encourage you to look at it.

You notice that all these primitives take as their last parameter the game scene. That's because any created mesh is added to the scene graph, in which the scene object is the root!

In our game, we will use boxes, spheres and torus to represent our objects. Later in this book, we will replace these objects with models created in a 3D computer graphic program (such as 3DS Max or Blender).

Good to know: layer masks

A layer mask (or culling mask in some 3d engines) is an attribute that can be used to selectively filter meshes on the camera's point of view. In Babylon.js, this attribute is a binary number: to select if an object has to be rendered on a camera, a simple logical AND is done between the mesh layer mask and the camera layer mask. If the result is greater or equals to 1, the object is rendered.

This feature can be used to hide some objects to a specific camera for example (like a minimap, or a GUI).

The following snippet sets a **layerMask** for all meshes of the scene:

```
scene.meshes.forEach(function(m) {
    m.layerMask = 1;
});
```

Cameras

There are a lot of cameras already defined in Babylon, and each has a specific use. You can create as many cameras as you want, but by default only one camera can be active at a time. If you want to have several cameras active at the same time, you will have to define a viewport for each one.

FreeCamera	The standard First Person Shooter camera
ArcRotateCamera	Rotates around a given point
TouchCamera	Camera used for touch devices
DeviceOrientationCamera	Move the camera by moving a mobile device
FollowCamera	Third Person Shooter camera. Follows a target.
VirtualJoysticksCamera	Creates two virtual joysticks on screen. Useful for mobile games
AnaglyphFreeCamera	FreeCamera dual view for red and cyan 3D glasses
AnaglyphArcRotateCamera	ArcRotateCamera dual view for red and cyan 3D glasses
GamepadCamera	Camera moving with a gamepad
VRDeviceOrientationFreeCamera	Orientation aware VR controller
WebVRFreeCamera	Camera for WebVR API

All cameras are described in the official documentation here: http://doc.babylonjs.com/tutorials/cameras.

In this game, we will use a FollowCamera as it is the camera that suits our gameplay the best.

The two most commonly used cameras are the FreeCamera and the ArcRotateCamera. Let's take some time to learn how to use them: you will learn several concepts used among all cameras in Babylon.

In order to use touch events, you need a polyfill library (such as hand.js available here https://github.com/deltakosh/handjs). Just include the library in your project and you're done!

FreeCamera

A FreeCamera is the standard FPS camera: you can move with it the arrow keys and rotate the view with the mouse. A FreeCamera belongs in the big family of TargetCamera, an abstract class above the FreeCamera and the FollowCamera.

The FreeCamera is also a super class for several other cameras, like the GamepadCamera, or the OculusCamera.

You can create a FreeCamera like this:

```
var camera = new BABYLON.FreeCamera(name, position, scene);
```

Here are several interesting attributes and methods for this type:

position	The camera's position in the world space.
rotation	The camera's rotation in the world space.
speed	The camera's movement speed. A high value means a high velocity.
keysUp keysDown keysLeft keysRight	Each attribute is an array containing key codes of each key moving the camera in this direction. Set to an empty array if you want to disable keyboard support.
attachControl(element)	Enables the camera control.
disableControl(element)	Disables the camera control.
setTarget(target)	Makes the camera look at the given target.
mode	Can be BABYLON.Camera.ORTHOGRAPHIC_CAMERA or BABYLON.Camera.PERSPECTIVE_CAMERA. Used to transform the camera in orthographic mode.
minZ maxZ	The camera's clipping space. Before minZ and after maxZ, the camera won't see anything.

There are a lot of other interesting and useful properties, but the ones in the table are the most commonly used. All others can be found in the official documentation.

ArcRotateCamera

An ArcRotateCamera is, as its name suggests, a camera that rotates around a point.

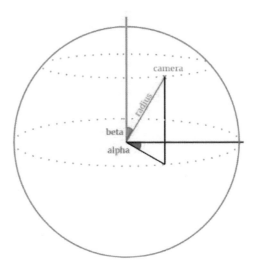

Figure 10 - The ArcRotateCamera behaviour

In the schema above, this camera is located on a sphere around its target. This sphere is defined by three parameters:

- Alpha: the red angle above, between the camera and Y-axis
- Beta: the green angle above, between the camera and X-axis
- Radius: the length between the camera and its target.

You can create an **ArcRotateCamera** like this:

```
var camera = new ArcRotateCamera(name, alpha, beta, radius, target, scene)
```

With controls activated, alpha and beta will change according to the mouse direction, but radius will stay constant. When zooming (with the mouse wheel or with two fingers on touch screens), alpha and beta will stay constant but radius will change.

Here are several interesting attributes and methods for this type:

alpha	The angle between the camera and Y-axis
beta	The angle between the camera and X-axis
radius	The radius of the arc rotate camera
target	Update the camera target (should be a Mesh or a Vector3)
lowerAlphaLimit upperAlphaLimit	The limit of the alpha angle. Useful to constrain the camera rotation between two angles.
lowerBetaLimit upperBetaLimit	Same as above but for the beta angle.
lowerRadiusLimit upperRadiusLimit	Same as above but for the camera radius.
keysUp keysDown keysLeft keysRight	Each attributes are arrays containing key codes of each key rotating the camera in this direction. Set to an empty array if you want to disable keyboard support.
attachControl(element)	Enables the camera control.
disableControl(element)	Disables the camera control.
setPosition(position)	Sets the camera to the given position. The target is unchanged, but alpha, beta and radius parameters are updated.

Lights

There are 4 types of lights in Babylon:

PointLight	Defined by a point, this lights emits in all directions
DirectionalLight	Emits in a specific direction. Can be used to make shadows.
SpotLight	Emits a cone shaped beam of light in a given direction. Can be used to make shadows.
HemisphericLight	Simulate the sun-light in a given direction

All lights are also described in the documentation here: http://doc.babylonjs.com/tutorials/lights.

In our game, we will use a hemispheric light to light the scene, and a directional light to create shadows.

In Babylon.js, PointLight, DirectionalLight and SpotLight can be used to create shadows.

HemisphericLight

A hemispheric light is the way to simulate a sky light. It is defined by the direction of the light and by its color.
Here is how to create a hemispheric light:

```
var light = new BABYLON.HemisphericLight(name, direction, scene);
```

The hemispheric light does not need to have a position set, as it simulates light at an infinite distance following the given direction.

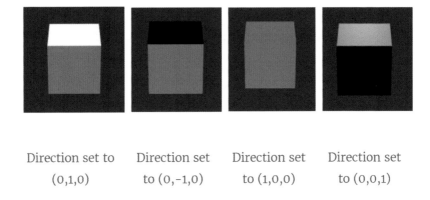

| Direction set to (0,1,0) | Direction set to (0,-1,0) | Direction set to (1,0,0) | Direction set to (0,0,1) |

Here are the important attributes and methods for this light:

diffuse	The light's color
specular	The light's specular color
groundColor	The color of the light on the ground (given by inverse direction of the light direction)
intensity	The light intensity. The larger this value is, the brighter this light will be.
excludedMeshes	An array of BABYLON.Mesh. All meshes in this array won't be lighted by this light.
includedOnlyMeshes	An array of BABYLON.Mesh. Only meshes in this array will be lighted by this light.

Please note that several properties are shared with other kind of lights (intensity, excludedMeshes, includedOnlyMeshes for example).

Below is an example of a sphere (without any material) lighted by a hemispheric light having the following properties:

- diffuse set to BABYLON.Color3.Red()
- specular set to BABYLON.Color3.Black()
- groundColor set to BABYLON.Color3.Blue()

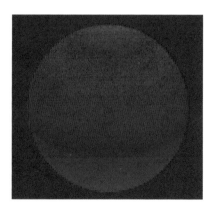

Clones and instances

Clone

In Babylon.js, each game object can be cloned via the method clone. Actually, this method works for several classes: mesh, vectors, quaternion, matrices, materials...

For most classes it works as a simple copy of the original object with the same values, but this behaviour is slightly different for meshes. Indeed, when you call the clone method on a mesh, like this:

```
var newMesh = mesh.clone("newName");
```

The geometry object (sharing all vertices, indices...) is exactly the same for both objects. It's interesting if you want to create a lot of similar objects and optimize memory.

Although all clones have the same underlying geometry object, they don't share the same material.

Instance

An instance of an object shares the same geometry of the original object and the same material. It is an excellent way to render a significant number of similar objects (an army, or a forest). Each instance has its own position, rotation and scaling, but shares the same material and geometry.

You can create an instance by calling the method createInstance:

```
var instance = mesh.createInstance("newName")
```

CHEAT SHEET

Babylon.js playground: http://www.babylonjs-playground.com/

Enable the debug layer:

```
scene.debugLayer.show();
```

Enable touch event with a polyfill:
https://github.com/deltakosh/handjs

Create a FreeCamera:

```
var camera = new BABYLON.FreeCamera(name, position, scene);
```

      name :   string ⇨ the camera name
      position: BABYLON.Vector3 ⇨ the camera position
      scene: BABYLON.Scene ⇨ the game scene.

The FreeCamera always looks along its own z-axis.

Create an ArcRotateCamera:

```
var camera = new ArcRotateCamera(name, alpha, beta, radius, target, scene)
```

      name :   string ⇨ the camera name
      alpha: number ⇨ the camera initial alpha angle
      beta: number ⇨ the camera initial beta angle
      radius: number ⇨ the camera initial radius
      target: BABYLON.Vector3 ⇨ the camera point of view
      scene: BABYLON.Scene ⇨ the game scene

Create a HemisphericLight:

```
var light = new BABYLON.HemisphericLight(name, direction, scene);
```

name: string ⇨ the light name

direction: BABYLON.Vector3 ⇨ the light direction

scene: BABYLON.Scene ⇨ the game scene

Cloning a mesh:

```
var newMesh = mesh.clone("newName");
```

Create an instance of a mesh:

```
var instance = mesh.createInstance("newName");
```

Differences between clones and instances: clones share their geometries, whereas instances share their geometries and materials.

CHAPTER 3 - DESIGN AND DEBUG YOUR GAME

While the other chapters of this book focus on the Babylon.js API, in this chapter we will present several useful tools and snippets of code to help you create, design and debug your game.

The playground

One of the biggest features of the Babylon.js world is without a doubt its playground.

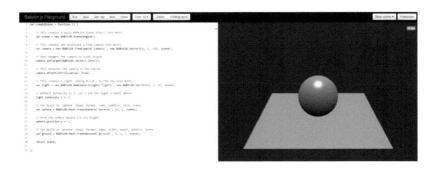

Figure 11 - The Babylon.js playground

This web application (available at http://www.babylonjs-playground.com/) is an experimenting platform, where you can write your own JavaScript code and directly check the result.

The whole Babylon.js API is directly embedded, and the result can be seen almost directly. The code panel on the left side of the screen is a smart editor based upon the Ace editor, shipped with an auto-completion for Babylon.js methods and classes.

The right panel is the rendering canvas where your result will be displayed. You can save your work and share it with a unique URL. You can also use the zip button to retrieve your project as a zip file, and use it as a working base for your game. Moreover, this playground is packaged with a lot of demos showing how to create specific features.

The only thing this playground asks of you is to have a method createScene that returns a new BABYLON.Scene.

Use it at will!

The debug layer

The debug layer is a new feature introduced in Babylon version 2.0. It gives you a fully functional UI to help you debug your game scene, with several useful tools:

- A mesh tree, to enable/disable meshes by name, and check how many vertices a mesh contains
- A statistics layer, to give you a global view about the engine performance
- Display objects bounding boxes
- Display a red overlay on mesh
- Activate/deactivate textures
- Display local axis for a mesh
- Display each mesh name

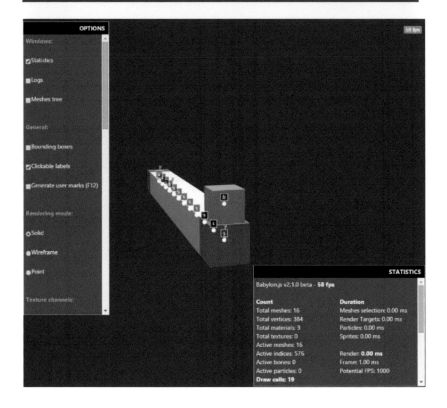

Figure 12 - The debug layer can show useful information

You can activate it anywhere you want in your project with only one line of code:

```
scene.debugLayer.show();
```

Don't forget to remove this line before moving into production ;)

The debug version of Babylon.js

In the official repository, several versions of Babylon.js can be found:

📄 babylon.2.5.js

📄 babylon.2.5.max.js

The only difference between these two versions is that the 'max' one is not minified: its source code can be browsed, read and understood. The second one is a minified version with all white characters removed, names updated...

During your game creation, I strongly encourage you to use the first version babylon.2.5.max.js. This way, all error messages returned by your browser will be understandable, and you will be able to quickly change your code and fix your mistakes.

Once your game is debugged and ready to move into production, you can switch to the minified version.

Show bounding box

In Babylon.js, each mesh has two bounding volumes that completely contain this mesh: a bounding box and a bounding sphere (this concept is detailed later in the book).

It is possible to display a bounding box for a given mesh, like this:

```
mesh.showBoundingBox = true;
```

Here is the bounding box displayed for two meshes (a cube and a sphere):

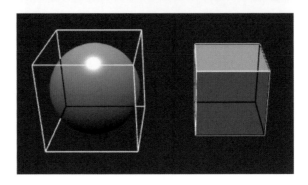

Pick and select an object

During your game creation, it can be useful to retrieve a mesh property, like its name, or its material name, by directly clicking on it.

Babylon.js provides several way of doing this, but an easy way is to define the method **onPointerDown** of the **BABYLON.Scene** object. An advantage of using this method is that all the magic is hidden: internally, a ray is fired from the mouse position to the 3D canvas, and the very first object intersecting with the ray is returned. With this method, you won't have to worry about creating and initializing the ray: just use it and get your result!

This function will be given two parameters: the DOM event, and a **BABYLON.PickingInfo** object. The code can be written like this:

```
scene.onPointerDown = function(evt, pickInfo) {
    // Your code here
};
```

A **PickingInfo** object has several interesting properties, as described below:

hit	True if the ray touched anything, false otherwise.
distance	The distance between the origin of the ray and the picked point.
pickedPoint	A Vector3 representing the intersecting point of the mesh.
pickedMesh	The instance of the mesh that intersects with this ray.
bu bv	Coordinates texture of the picked points.

This object will also be used in a next chapter (CHAPTER 11 – Collisions and actions).

Outline a mesh

Sometimes it can be useful to highlight a specific mesh to make it easy to identify. It's very easy to do so in Babylon:

```
var sphere = BABYLON.Mesh.CreateSphere("sphere1", 16, 2, scene);
sphere.renderOutline = true;
sphere.outlineWidth = 0.1;
sphere.outlineColor = BABYLON.Color3.Yellow();
```

The attribute renderOutline set to true will draw a default red outline around your mesh. The following attribute (outlineWidth and outlineColor) can be used to configure the rendered outline. Here is the result corresponding to this code:

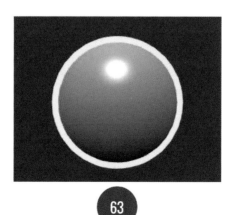

Screen coordinates to world coordinates

Sometimes, it may be useful to display some 2D information above a specific mesh: the number of lives for a specific player, or any metadata linked to a 3D object. For this data, the 2D object can be represented by a DOM object: such as an HTML division or image.

In this case, you have to convert a 3D position (or a world coordinate) (x, y, z) into a 2D position (or a screen coordinate) (x, y).

Babylon.js provides a simple method to do so:

> – Converting 3D to 2D to get a screen position is called Project
> – Converting 2D to 3D to get a world position is called Unproject

Project into 2D world

Here is how to use the Project method:

```
// Update the scene transformation matrix
scene.updateTransformMatrix();

// 3D position
var _3Dposition = new BABYLON.Vector3(10, 10, 10);

// Projection from 3D to 2D
var _2Dposition = BABYLON.Vector3.Project(
  _3Dposition,
  BABYLON.Matrix.Identity(),          // World matrix
  scene.getTransformMatrix(),         // Transformation matrix
  scene.activeCamera.viewport.toGlobal(engine) // Viewport
);
div.style.top = _2Dposition.y+"px";
div.style.left = _2Dposition.x+"px";
```

The first line `scene.updateTransformMatrix()` is mandatory in order to compute the scene transformation matrix, which is used in the Project method.

A transformation matrix is a matrix
representing all operations needed to convert
one space to another.

Finally, the HTML division position is updated according to the result
returned by the Project method.

Unproject into 3D world

Here is how to use the Unproject method:

```
// The screen position is updated during mousemove
var _2Dposition = new BABYLON.Vector3();
window.addEventListener("click", function(evt) {
  // The position is updated according to the canvas size
  var canvas_rect = engine.getRenderingCanvasClientRect();
  _2Dposition.x = (evt.clientX - canvas_rect.left) / canvas_rect.width;
  _2Dposition.y = (evt.clientY - canvas_rect.top) / canvas_rect.height;
});

// Unproject returns a position in the 3D world
var _3Dposition = BABYLON.Vector3.Unproject(
  _2Dposition.clone(),        // The mouse position is duplicated
  camera.viewport.width,      // the camera field of view (width value)
  camera.viewport.height,     // the camera field of view (height value)
  BABYLON.Matrix.Identity(),  // World matrix where the projection wille be
done.
  camera.getViewMatrix(),     // The camera view matrix
  camera.getProjectionMatrix() // The camera projection matrix
);
```

CHAPTER 4 - WORKING WITH CLASSES

We will build our game by creating classes for each entity. This chapter describes all classes we need to create and presents their implementations. All class should be in their own Javascript file, and included in your HTML file in order to run correctly.

The Game class

Game
+ engine : BABYLON.Engine
+ scene : BABYLON.Scene
+ assets : []
+ currentLevel : number
- _initScene
- _initGame
+ nextLevel
+ reset

Figure 13 - The game class

Game constructor

In the constructor, all members are initialized to their default value, and most importantly the Babylon engine is created. The scene is also initialized, and the game render loop is defined.

In the next chapter, when external resources (3D models) will be loaded into our game, a loading part will be needed. This loading part will be in the game constructor (but not now, one step at a time ☺).

```javascript
window.addEventListener("DOMContentLoaded", function() {
  new Game("gameCanvas");
}, false);

var Game = function(canvasId) {
  var canvas  = document.getElementById(canvasId);
  this.engine = new BABYLON.Engine(canvas, true);

  // BABYLON Scene creation
  this.scene  = this._initScene(this.engine);

  // Contains all 3D models
  this.assets = [];

  // The current level
  this.currentLevel = 1;

  // The player object
  this.player = null;

  // The level being played
  this.level = null;

  // Init the game
  this._initGame();

  var _this = this;
  this.engine.runRenderLoop(function () {
    _this.scene.render();
  });
};
```

Scene initialization

The method _initScene will create the game scene, and create the default camera, the default light... Everything that will not change during the game goes in this method.

Here, a FreeCamera is used to create our game, but we will change it later to use a FollowCamera.

The FreeCamera is great when building your scene, as you can move freely in your virtual world.

```
Game.prototype._initScene = function(engine) {
  // BABYLON Scene creation
  var scene  = new BABYLON.Scene(engine);
  // The camera, necessary see the world
  var camera = new BABYLON.FreeCamera("camera", new BABYLON.Vector3(2.5,6,-6.5), scene);
  camera.rotation = new BABYLON.Vector3(Math.PI/3.5, 0, 0);
  camera.attachControl(engine.getRenderingCanvas());

  // The ambient light
  var light  = new BABYLON.HemisphericLight("light", new BABYLON.Vector3(0,1,0), scene);
  light.intensity = 0.7;

  return scene;
};
```

The method camera.attachControl takes the game canvas as a parameter and enable the camera control in the game. It is that easy!

The method camera.detachControl exists for the reverse operation.

Game initialization

Two new objects are created:

- A Player object: the ball
- A Level object: creates all game blocks, add keys, spikes, and sets the start and finish position.

```
Game.prototype._initGame = function() {
    // The player object
    this.player = new Player(this);

    // Level creation from... ints ? wtf !
    this.level = Level.FromInts(levels[this.currentLevel], this);

    // The player position is set to the start position of the level ..
    this.player.position = this.level.start.position.clone();
    // ... but slightly above it.
    this.player.position.y = 2;

    // Activate the debug Layer
    this.scene.debugLayer.show();
};
```

You can see a new level is created from an array named levels... but we will see it just after the Player class. And I cannot tell you about the Player without presenting the GameObject class first... so let's try to do it in order.

The entity base class: GameObject

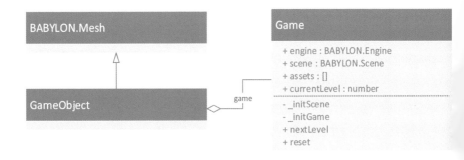

Figure 14 - The GameObject class

The GameObject class will be our game entities' base class. It will directly extends the class BABYLON.Mesh in order to ease the manipulation of all sub-objects. Again, don't forget to include GameObject.js in your HTML file.

```javascript
var GameObject = function(name, game) {
  // Call the super class BABYLON.Mesh
  BABYLON.Mesh.call(this, name, game.scene);

  this.game = game;
  this.scene = game.scene;
};

// Our object is a BABYLON.Mesh
GameObject.prototype = Object.create(BABYLON.Mesh.prototype);
// And its constructor is the GameObject function described above.
GameObject.prototype.constructor = GameObject;
```

If you create a GameObject, you won't see anything, because this class has no geometry. It is the equivalent of a Game Object in Unity, or a dummy in 3DSMax, and will only be used to control other complex models with a parent-child relationship.

In Babylon, you can have a parent-child relationship between two objects like this:

```javascript
mesh.parent = otherMesh;
```

This link means that all transformations made to the parent object will be applied to the child. Be careful: all transformations made to the children won't be applied to the parent.

A mesh can have several child objects, but it can have only one parent. Why is it useful? Let's take a concrete example. Imagine you have a simple character, with several meshes: a head, a body, two arms and two legs. How do you make it move? One solution could be to do this:

```javascript
head.position.x += speed;
body.position.x += speed;
```

```
arms1.position.x += speed;
arms2.position.x += speed;
leg1.position.x += speed;
leg2.position.x += speed;
```

But it's not very easy to manipulate. What if you want to make it rotate?

A second solution is to link all parts of the character to a GameObject, and then manipulate the GameObject:

```
var character = new GameObject();
head.parent = character;
body.parent = character;
arms1.parent = character;
arms2.parent = character;
leg1.parent = character;
leg2.parent = character;

character.position.x += speed;
character.rotation.x += Math.PI/2;
```

Now, we can introduce the Player class ☺

The player class

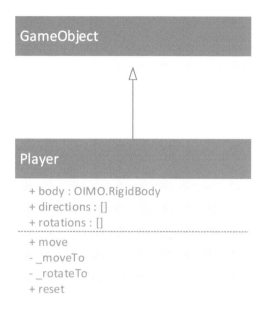

Figure 15 - Our Player class

First thing to note: the Player extends the GameObject class. In Javascript, as there is no class implementation per se, the Player prototype will be based on the GameObject prototype.

But in the code, the Player constructor does something strange with a VertexData object... See for yourself:

```
var Player = function (game) {
GameObject.call(this, "player", game);

// The physics body (see later)
this.body = null;
// The player can move in two directions...
this.directions = [0,0];
// ...and rotate in two directions
this.rotations = [0,0];

// Let's give this player a spherical shape
var vertexData = BABYLON.VertexData.CreateSphere(16, 0.75,
BABYLON.Mesh.DEFAULTSIDE);
vertexData.applyToMesh(this);
```

```
// The player position is above the ground
this.position.y = Player.START_HEIGHT;

// Save this for later
var _this = this;
this.getScene().registerBeforeRender(function() {
  if (_this.position.y < -10) {
    _this.game.reset();
  }
});
};

// Our object is a GameObject
Player.prototype = Object.create(GameObject.prototype);
Player.prototype.constructor = Player;
```

In all 3D engines, a mesh geometry is internally represented by a list of vertices (and many other parameters).

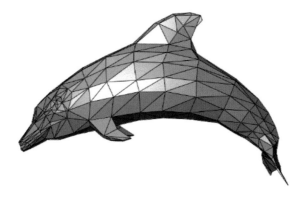

Figure 16 - Example of a dolphin mesh. Each point is a vertex.

In Babylon.js, a VertexData object is the main component of a mesh geometry. It contains members (among others) like vertices positions, normal, uv, indices. The method BABYLON.VertexData.CreateSphere is used to create a sphere geometry, that is then applied to the mesh. Our player is thus a sphere mesh!

Levels

Level data structure

A level is composed of several blocks aligned along the x-axis and z-axis.

Figure 17 - Example of a level without any keys or spikes. The sphere is the player.

The player starts at a given position, and should reach a final position. On his path, spikes can prevent him from moving: the player should get the corresponding key to remove the spikes and move forward.

In our virtual world, the player, the key and the spike block will be represented by specific 3D models (created in 3DSMax), and all block will be made with the Box primitive of Babylon.js.

In order to create levels easily, we will use a simple matrix representation (a two-dimensional array) where each element of the level (spikes and keys) is a simple character or a number:

- S represents the starting position
- F is the finish position
- 0 represents an empty block
- \- is no block at all
- Any number represents a spike
- The same negative number is the corresponding key.

An example of a correct level could be this:

```
[
  ['S',0,0,0,-1,0,0,0,0,1,'F']
];
```

Or this:

```
[
  ['S',0 ,0 ,0 ,-1 ,'-'],
  [1 ,'-', '-','-','-','-'],
  [0 ,'-',0 ,0 ,-2 ,'-'],
  [0 ,0 ,0 ,'-','-','-'],
  ['-','-',2 ,0 ,0 ,'F']
];
```

Our Level class will read this and create a 3D level accordingly.

Class diagram

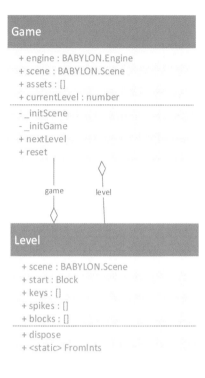

Figure 18 - The Level class

Nothing complicated here: a Level instance stores an instance of the Game, in order to access to the game scene. Note that every key or spike, and all blocks are stored in arrays, in order to properly remove them from the scene when the level is finished.

Don't forget to keep a reference to your BABYLON.Mesh in order to remove them properly and avoid memory leaks.

Let's check the code:

```
var Level = function(game) {
  this.scene = game.scene;
  this.game = game;
```

```javascript
// The starting position in this level
this.start = null;

// Each keys of the current level
this.keys = [];

// Each spikes of the current level
this.spikes = [];

// The level blocks
this.blocks = [];
};

/**
 * Delete the current level
 */
Level.prototype.dispose = function() {
  this.blocks.forEach(function(b) {
    b.dispose();
  });

  this.keys.forEach(function(k) {
    k.delete();
  });
};
```

Level creation

The method FromInts is a static function, taking as a parameter a level matrix (as described above) and an instance of a Game, to return a new level corresponding to the matrix. Here is the corresponding code:

```javascript
/**
 * Creates a new map from a matrix of ints
 */
Level.FromInts = function(matrix, game) {

  var level = new Level(game);

  for (var z=0; z<matrix.length; z++) {
    for (var x=0; x<matrix[z].length; x++) {
```

```javascript
var type = matrix[z][x];
var block = null;
if (type == Block.TYPES.NOTHING) {
  // Nothing to do here
} else {
  // Creates a block
  block = new Block(x, z, game);
  level.blocks.push(block);
  if (type == Block.TYPES.NORMAL) {
    // Useless to do more
  } else if (type == Block.TYPES.START) {
    level.start = block;
  } else if (type == Block.TYPES.FINISH) {
    var a = new Apple(game);
    a.position = block.position.clone();
    a.position.y = 1;
    level.finish = block;
  } else {
    // this block is a spike or a key
    if (type > 0) {
      // It's a spike
      var s = new Spikes(game, Math.abs(type));
      s.position = new BABYLON.Vector3(x, 0.5, -z);
      level.spikes.push(s);
    } else {
      // It's a key
      var k = new Key(game, Math.abs(type));
      k.position = new BABYLON.Vector3(x, 0.75, -z);
      level.keys.push(k);
    }
  }
}
}

//For all keys, link it to its spike
for (var k=0; k<level.keys.length; k++) {
  var currentKey = level.keys[k];
  for (var s=0; s<level.spikes.length; s++) {
    var currentSpike = level.spikes[s];

    if (currentSpike.number == currentKey.number) {
      currentKey.link(currentSpike);
    }
  }
}
```

```
  return level;
};
```

This method uses 4 new objects:
- A Block object
- A Spike object
- A Key object
- An Apple object

Let's start with the Block class.

The Block class

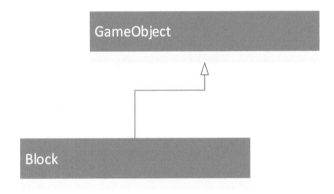

Figure 19 - The Block class

There is nothing you cannot understand here, as it is very similar to the Player class, and no new concept is introduced. Just pay attention to the shape this element is given:

```
var Block = function (x, z, game) {
  GameObject.call(this, "block", game);
  var vertexData = BABYLON.VertexData.CreateBox(1,
BABYLON.Mesh.DEFAULTSIDE);
  vertexData.applyToMesh(this);

  this.position.x = x;
```

```
  this.position.z = -z;
};

// Our object is a GameObject
Block.prototype = Object.create(GameObject.prototype);
// And its constructor is the Block function described above.
Block.prototype.constructor = Block;

Block.TYPES = {
  NOTHING : '-',
  NORMAL : 0,
  START : 'S',
  FINISH : 'F'
};
```

The Key class

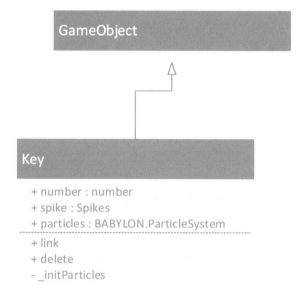

Figure 20 - The Key class

A Key extends the GameObject class, as it is a 3D element in the level. The new thing is the number attribute (which is a constructor parameter too). This number will be used by the Level class to "link" the key to its corresponding spike block. This way, if the player takes a key, the Key instance will be able to deactivate its spike block.

We will see later how the sentence 'the player takes a key' can be translated in the Babylon world with the collision system.

```javascript
var Key = function(game, number) {
    // Call the super class BABYLON.Mesh
    GameObject.call(this, "key", game);

    this.number = number;
    this.spike = null;

    var key = BABYLON.Mesh.CreateTorus("key", 0.75, 0.25, 10, this.getScene());
    key.parent = this;

};
// Our object is a GameObject
Key.prototype = Object.create(GameObject.prototype);
// And its constructor is the Key function described above.
Key.prototype.constructor = Key;

Key.prototype.link = function(spike) {
    this.spike = spike;
};

/**
 * Delete this key from the world
 */
Key.prototype.delete = function() {
    this.spike.delete();
    this.dispose();
};
```

But wait... Why not give it a shape, like we did to the Block class (with a BABYLON.VertexData object)? This is because a key will be later (in the next chapter) replaced with a complex 3D model made in 3DSMax. As the complex model cannot be summed up as a single geometry, the parent-child relation is the best thing to do here.

The Spike class

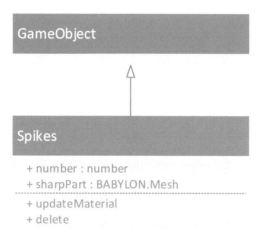

Figure 21 - The Spike class

The **Spike** class is nothing really complicated right now. The number attribute is the same as in the Key class, and the **sharpPart** attribute is something that is being used in the **updateMaterial** method.

When a key is linked to a Spike object, the key material will also be applied to the spike, for the player to see easily which key is linked to which spike.

You might ask what a material is... And the answer is in the next chapter!

```
var Spikes = function(game, number) {
  GameObject.call(this, "spikes", game);

  this.number = number;
  this.sharpPart = BABYLON.Mesh.CreateCylinder("cylinder", 0.5, 0.5, 0.5, 6, 1,
  this.getScene());
  this.sharpPart.parent = this;

};
```

```
// Our object is a GameObject
Spikes.prototype = Object.create(GameObject.prototype);
// And its constructor is the Spikes function described above.
Spikes.prototype.constructor = Spikes;

Spikes.prototype.updateMaterial = function(mat) {
  this.sharpPart.material = mat;
};

Spikes.prototype.delete = function() {
  this.dispose();
};
```

The Apple class

Finally, the last class of our game, representing the finish block: the Apple!

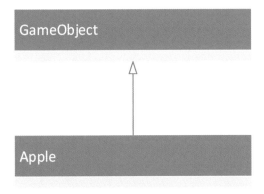

Figure 22 - The Apple class

There is absolutely nothing to explain here... Right now, our Apple is nothing but a torus knot. It will be more interesting in the next chapter ☺

```
var Apple = function(game) {
  // Call the super class BABYLON.Mesh
```

```
GameObject.call(this, "apple", game);

var apple = BABYLON.Mesh.CreateTorusKnot("knot", 0.25, 0.05, 64, 64, 2, 3,
this.getScene());

apple.parent = this;
};
// Our object is a GameObject
Apple.prototype = Object.create(GameObject.prototype);
// And its constructor is the Key function described above.
Apple.prototype.constructor = Apple;
```

Here is what you should see when running index.html. Nothing really fancy, as we could imagine.

In the next chapter, we will learn how to apply some colors to our game.

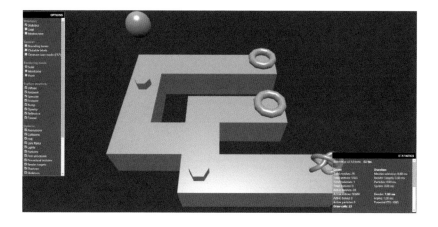

Figure 23 - Your game with basic shapes

CHAPTER 5 - MATERIALS

In this chapter, we will talk (a lot!) about materials. We will first explain how you can customize them, and then apply all this knowledge to our game.

The default material

A material defines the optical properties of an object: basically its color and its shininess. Mathematically, this corresponds to a set of coefficients describing how the light interacts with the object surface. There are many parameters to play with on a material, and knowing them will help you to create the best atmosphere to suit your game.

> In Babylon.js, a material is a node of the scene graph, and thus can be applied to several objects at the same time.

You can create a material with one line of code:

```
var material = new BABYLON.StandardMaterial("myFirstMaterial", scene);
```

The material is created with a name and added to the scene graph. You should now apply it to a given mesh. Let's take a sphere for example:

```
var sphere = BABYLON.Mesh.CreateSphere("sphere1", 16, 2, scene);
sphere.material = material;
```

And that's it! The node (material) is applied to the sphere with the second line.

The material you just created is the default standard material. It's a shiny greyish color, as it is shown in the Figure 24 below).

You surely noticed applying the material didn't do anything special to the sphere... That's because under normal circumstances, an object without any material is rendered with a default standard material.

Figure 24 - The default material

Now, let's try to add some colors.

Colors

There are 2 objects representing colors in Babylon.js:
- BABYLON.Color3
- BABYLON.Color4

Each color has 3 attributes corresponding to the red value, blue value and green value. The last parameter of a Color4 is the alpha value. Just remember that all the following attributes for a material need a Color3 object.

There are a few colors already defined in Babylon. Each of the functions below returns a new instance of a Color3 object:

```
BABYLON.Color3.Red()
BABYLON.Color3.Green()
BABYLON.Color3.Blue()
BABYLON.Color3.Black()
BABYLON.Color3.White()
BABYLON.Color3.Purple()
BABYLON.Color3.Magenta()
BABYLON.Color3.Yellow()
BABYLON.Color3.Gray()
```

Roses are red, violets are blue

Do you want colors? I will help you.

After this short poem, let's see all attributes of a StandardMaterial at our disposal to apply some colors.

Diffuse color

The diffuse color of an object is the color the object reveals under white light. The final color of the material will therefore be affected by the light intensity and by the light color.

```
material.diffuseColor = new BABYLON.Color3(1,0,0);
```

Specular color

The specular color is the color of the bright spot of light appearing on shiny object. If the specular color is set to black, the bright spot disappears and the object has a matte aspect.

The specular spot can be adjusted with the parameter specularPower

```
material.specularColor = new BABYLON.Color3(1,1,1);
material.specularPower = 8;
```

diffuseColor: new BABYLON.Color3(1, 0, 0);
specularColor: new BABYLON.Color3(1, 1, 1);

diffuseColor: new BABYLON.Color3(1, 0, 0);
specularColor: new BABYLON.Color3(0,0,0);

Figure 25 - With and without specular color

Ambient color

The ambient color can be seen as a second level of diffuse color, but relatively to the scene's ambient color. By default, the scene's ambient color is set to black, so this value should be updated beforehand. You can notice in Figure 26 below that the red is darker at the bottom of the sphere. That is not the case with an emissive color.

```
var material = new BABYLON.StandardMaterial("", scene);
scene.ambientColor = new BABYLON.Color3(1,1,1);
material.ambientColor = new BABYLON.Color3(0.5,0,0);
```

Without ambient color

scene.ambientColor = new
BABYLON.Color3(1,1,1);
material.ambientColor = new
BABYLON.Color3(0.5,0,0);

Figure 26 – With and without ambient color

Emissive color

The emissive color is the color of the object without any light source. It can be seen as the color emitted by the object.

```
material.emissiveColor = BABYLON.Color3.White();
```

Without emissive color

material.emissiveColor = BABYLON.Color3.Red();

Figure 27 - With and without emissive color

Textures

In 3d, a texture is 2D image applied on a 3D mesh to add some details or colors. You can think of it like wrapping paper. Texture can be static (standard images) or defined procedurally (procedural textures). This chapter will only describe static textures.

Textures should be applied on a StandardMaterial, like colors have been set. All supported formats include:

- JPEG .jpg
- Graphics Interchange Format .gif
- Portable Network Graphics .png
- TARGA .tga
- DirectDraw Surface .dds

The Texture object

To set a texture to an object, you will have to create a BABYLON.Texture. This object has several interesting properties.

hasAlpha	Should be set to true if the texture has alpha parts.
uOffset vOffset	The offset of the texture
uScale vScale	The number of times the texture should be repeated
uAng vAng wAng	The texture's rotation

Babylon.js can handle all sizes of textures, but a texture whose size is a power of two is best handled in memory.

Diffuse texture

Here is the code to add a diffuse texture. As the diffuse color, the diffuse texture will react to the light the object receives.

```
var groundMat = new BABYLON.StandardMaterial("ground",scene);
groundMat.diffuseTexture = new BABYLON.Texture("assets/ground4.jpg",scene);
box.material = groundMat;
```

Original texture   Texture applied on diffuseTexture

Texture applied on diffuseTexture   Texture applied on diffuseTexture

+   +

emissiveColor set to white   emissiveColor set to green

As shown above, color properties and texture properties can be mixed to produce a material that suits your needs.

Emissive texture

Like the emissive color, an emissive texture is the texture of the object without any light source. Here is how to use it:

```
material.emissiveTexture = new BABYLON.Texture("emissive.png", scene);
sphere.material = material;
```

Below are two images with the same texture applied on the emissive and diffuse channels:

Emissive texture only   Diffuse texture only

Ambient texture

An ambient texture can be used to display light maps.

```
var groundMat = new BABYLON.StandardMaterial("ground",scene);
groundMat.diffuseTexture = new BABYLON.Texture("assets/ground5.jpg",scene);
groundMat.ambientTexture = new
BABYLON.Texture("assets/ground5LM.jpg",scene);
box.material = groundMat;
```

| Diffuse texture | Ambient texture | Result |

Specular texture

The specular texture describes how the specular spot will look like.

```
var groundMat = new BABYLON.StandardMaterial("ground",scene);
groundMat.specularTexture = new BABYLON.Texture("assets/ground4.jpg",scene);
box.material = groundMat;
```

Bump texture

A bump texture can be used to simulate bumps and wrinkles on the surface of an object. In the example below, notice how the bump texture makes the ground less smooth, and how the white highlight disappears with the specular texture.

| Diffuse texture only | Diffuse texture + Bump texture | Diffuse texture + Bump texture + Specular texture |

Here is how to use a bump texture:

```
material.bumpTexture = new BABYLON.Texture("bump.png", scene);
sphere.material = material;
```

Opacity texture

Opacity texture can be used to define precisely an object transparency. Be careful, if your opacity texture has no alpha channel, you have to set the property getAlphaFromRGB to true. By default, the specular will be applied to transparent parts (like an empty glass). To disable this behavior, just set the property useSpecularOverAlpha to false.

```
var groundMat = new BABYLON.StandardMaterial("ground",scene);
groundMat.opacityTexture = new BABYLON.Texture("assets/ground4O.jpg",scene);
groundMat.opacityTexture.getAlphaFromRGB = true;
box.material = groundMat;
```

Opacity texture	With opacity texture + getAlphaFromRGB = true	With opacity texture + useSpecularOverAlpha = false;

Reflection texture

A reflection texture can be used to simulate reflecting objects, or to give a shiny metal aspect to an object. It is only a simulation, not a real mirror.

A StandardMaterial has the attribute reflectionTexture that takes a BABYLON.Texture as a parameter (like diffuseTexture for example). Two kinds of textures can be used, with several different results:

    - a simple texture, which has its attribute coordinatesMode set to:

        - BABYLON.Texture.SPHERICAL_MODE

        - BABYLON.Texture.CUBIC_MODE

        - BABYLON.Texture.PLANAR_MODE

        - BABYLON.Texture.PROJECTION_MODE

    - a cube texture

Here is the code corresponding to a reflection texture set in spherical mode:

```
var material = new BABYLON.StandardMaterial("reflectionMat", scene);
material.reflectionTexture = new BABYLON.Texture("textures/misc.jpg", scene);
material.reflectionTexture.coordinatesMode =
BABYLON.Texture.SPHERICAL_MODE;
myMesh.material = material;
```

A cube texture is a specific kind of texture composed of 6 images (see next chapter Skybox)

Here is the code corresponding to this specific reflection:

```
material = new BABYLON.StandardMaterial("cubeReflectionMat", scene);
// The name of the cube texture is the image name without any suffixes
material.reflectionTexture = new BABYLON.CubeTexture("skybox", scene);
myMesh.material = material;
```

A cube texture can also have its attribute coordinatesMode updated (set to cubic mode by default).

For a reflection texture, the coordinate mode must be set in order to be displayed.

Figure 28 - Example of a reflection texture on a plane

Small talk about draw calls

A good metaphor to explain draw calls would comparing it to a painter's point of view. A draw call is similar to when a painter has to unload his brush with one color before loading up the next one. Here, we are talking about materials: the more material your scene has, the more draw calls you will have. A lot of draw calls can drastically reduce your performance, so be careful when manipulating a lot of materials!

In Babylon.js, a material object is a node in the scene graph, so it can be applied to several meshes without impacting performance. A good practice is then to create only one material, and apply it everywhere.

Remember: a lot of materials decrease performance. Keep the total number of material objects low, and everything will be alright ☺

98

Performance can also be decreased if your texture sizes are too big. Keep in mind that all textures are loaded in memory!

Fresnel parameters

The Fresnel effect is the observation that the amount of reflectance you can see on a surface depends of the viewing angle. For example, you will see more reflected light if you look at a swimming pool with your eye at the water level than if you look straight down from above. This Fresnel effect can be adjusted with the Fresnel parameters provided by Babylon.js. There are 4 of them:

```
material.diffuseFresnelParameters = new BABYLON.FresnelParameters();
material.opacityFresnelParameters = new BABYLON.FresnelParameters();
material.reflectionFresnelParameters = new BABYLON.FresnelParameters();
material.emissiveFresnelParameters = new BABYLON.FresnelParameters();
```

The Fresnel effect will be applied on the corresponding channel (diffuse, opacity, reflection and/or emissive), and change the color/texture is applied on the mesh according to the camera's point of view.

A FresnelParameters object has few attributes, but all are of interest:

isEnabled	True or false: activate or deactivate the effect
leftColor	Defines the color used on edges.
rightColor	Defines the color used on the center.
bias	Number used to compute the Fresnel term.
power	Number used to compute the Fresnel term.

We will apply it to our player in a few paragraphs.

Back to our game!

Wow! That was a long theory section here, but that's because materials are fundamental in your scene's realism: knowing how to manipulate colors and textures is vital in immersing the player as much as possible in your game.

Set a texture to our blocks

As there may be a lot of blocks in a level, we will create only one material and apply it to all our block objects.

First, choose a ground texture, create a folder 'assets' in your project and save the texture in this folder.

Figure 29 - The ground texture

The code should be set in the Level class when the level is created:

```
var groundMat = new BABYLON.StandardMaterial("ground", game.scene);
groundMat.diffuseTexture = new BABYLON.Texture("assets/ground4.jpg",
game.scene);
```

And when a block object is created:

```
block.material = groundMat;
```

And that's it! You can run your project now to see some beautiful ground.

Don't hesitate to tweak the values to create the ground that suits your taste.

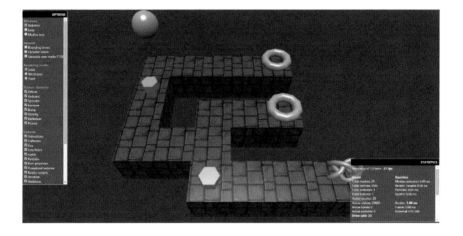

Figure 30 - Our first level with a beautiful ground

The player material

For the player, we want something transparent in the center, but colored on the edges: it's a perfect situation for using Fresnel parameters!

First, we should create a transparent material, like this:

```
var material = new BABYLON.StandardMaterial("playerMaterial", this.getScene());
material.diffuseColor = new BABYLON.Color3(1,1,1);
material.emissiveColor = new BABYLON.Color3(1,1,1);
material.alpha = 0.1;
```

Figure 31 - The player material v1.0

Now, let's add some Fresnel effects.

```
var array = randomColor({luminosity: 'light', hue:'red', format:'rgbArray'});
var color = BABYLON.Color3.FromInts(array[0], array[1], array[2]);

material.emissiveFresnelParameters = new BABYLON.FresnelParameters();
material.emissiveFresnelParameters.bias = 0.6;
material.emissiveFresnelParameters.power = 2;
material.emissiveFresnelParameters.leftColor = BABYLON.Color3.Black();
material.emissiveFresnelParameters.rightColor = color;

material.opacityFresnelParameters = new BABYLON.FresnelParameters();
material.opacityFresnelParameters.leftColor = BABYLON.Color3.White();
material.opacityFresnelParameters.rightColor = BABYLON.Color3.Black();
```

I use the awesome library **randomColor** created by David Merfield
(available here: http://llllll.li/randomColor/) to generate a different
color (only one constraint: red hue) each time the game is launched.
Finally, don't forget to link the material to the player:

```
this.material = material;
```

Indeed, as our Player instance is a Mesh instance, the attribute
this.material can be used.
And here we are!

Figure 32 – The Player material v2.0

Skybox

In games, a skybox is a wrapper around your entire scene that shows what the world look like. Technically, it's a box with each face corresponding to a different texture.

This texture is called a CubeTexture, and is composed of 6 images. Each image should have the same base name and the same extension, and each name should correspond to a cube face: px, py, pz for images along axis x, y, z, and nx, ny, nz for images along axis –x, -y, -z.

Figure 33 - Example of a skybox

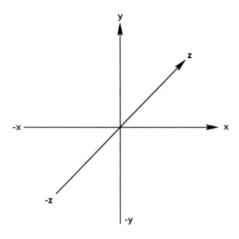

Figure 34 - Axis used for a skybox

Here is the code to create such a skybox in Babylon.js. This code should be in the method initScene of our Game class, as it is something that will never be updated:

```
var skybox = BABYLON.Mesh.CreateBox("skyBox", 100.0, scene);
var skyboxMaterial = new BABYLON.StandardMaterial("skyBox", scene);
skyboxMaterial.backFaceCulling = false;
skyboxMaterial.reflectionTexture = new
BABYLON.CubeTexture("assets/skybox/TropicalSunnyDay", scene);
skyboxMaterial.reflectionTexture.coordinatesMode =
BABYLON.Texture.SKYBOX_MODE;
skyboxMaterial.diffuseColor = new BABYLON.Color3(0, 0, 0);
skyboxMaterial.specularColor = new BABYLON.Color3(0, 0, 0);
skybox.material = skyboxMaterial;
```

Don't forget to copy your skybox images into your project ☺

Figure 35 - Our game scene with all materials

Much better looking than in the previous chapter, don't you think?

Shadows

In any 3D scene, shadows add another level of depth and realism since they can transform something that looks flat into something that looks more three dimensional.

In Babylon.js, only directional lights and spot lights can cast shadows. The light is then used to create a shadow map, which should be updated with all object casting shadows.

> When creating shadows, the light must have a position set in order to give to Babylon.js its point of view.

105

Let's update our Game class (method initScene):

```
var dl = new BABYLON.DirectionalLight("dir", new BABYLON.Vector3(1,-1,-0.5),
scene);
dl.position = new BABYLON.Vector3(0, 40, 0);
this.shadows = new BABYLON.ShadowGenerator(1024, dl);
this.shadows.useBlurVarianceShadowMap = true;
```

The first parameter of the ShadowGenerator is the size of the shadow map (should be power-of-two). For good performance, keep this number low, or high if you want precise shadows.

The last line is used to activate a shadow filter. There are 3 filters available:

    – Variance shadow map:

        –shadowGenerator.useVarianceShadowMap = true

    – Poisson sampling:

        – shadowGenerator.usePoissonSampling = true

    – Blur variance shadow map:

        – shadowGenerator.useBlurVarianceShadowMap = true;

In order for another mesh to receive a shadow, a specific attribute should be set:

```
mesh.receiveShadows = true;
```

Don't forget to activate shadows for transparent objects:

```
this.shadows.setTransparencyShadow(true);
```

Let's apply this to our blocks (in the Block class constructor):

```
this.receiveShadows = true;
```

Now, let's use the shadow map we created to render some shadows. Let's take the Key class for example. Add this in its constructor:

```
game.shadows.getShadowMap().renderList.push(key);
```

And that's it! Here, the shadow map of the `ShadowGenerator` object is retrieved, and a mesh is pushed into its list of objects to render. Try to do this for all kinds of mesh in the game (except blocks obviously). Here is what you should see afterwards:

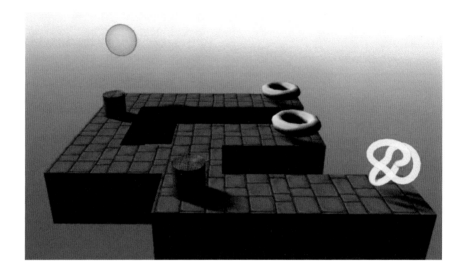

Figure 36 - The game with shadows

Multi-material

A multi-material lets you assign different materials to different parts of the same object. Your object will be separated into sub meshes, identified by a set of vertices and a set of indices.

Basically, a multi-material is just an array of standard materials: first, you have to create all your materials (assign colors, textures...) in order to add them in your multi-material object.

You can create a multi-material object like this:

```
var multimat = new BABYLON.MultiMaterial("multimat", scene);
```

Then, add all your standard materials:

```
multimat.subMaterials.push(standardmat1);
multimat.subMaterials.push(standardmat2);
multimat.subMaterials.push(standardmat3);
```

Your simple materials should be pushed only once in this array. Finally, set your material to your mesh:

```
cube.material = multimat;
```

By default, only the first material is used by the mesh, because all meshes are created with only one sub-mesh (corresponding to the whole mesh). In order to apply all materials, you can define sub-meshes like this:

```
cube.subMeshes = [];
var submesh1 = new BABYLON.SubMesh(0, vertexStart, vertexCount, indiceStart, indiceCount, mesh);
cube.subMeshes.push(submesh1);
```

A BABYLON.SubMesh is created with the following parameters:
- The sub-material index to use for this sub-mesh, relative to the multi-material object.
- The sub-mesh starts at vertexStart and has vertexCount vertices.
- Same as above but for indices.
- The mesh this sub-mesh should be applied on.

This kind of object is used a lot when 3D models are created by programs like 3DS Max, Maya or Blender, and it is useful to know how to use them.

Exercise

Try to create other materials for the Key class, Spike class and Apple class. Be creative, and try experimenting with all the parameters that were explained previously. The previous image shows an example of the scene you could create.

CHEAT SHEET

Create a new StandardMaterial and affect it to a mesh:

```
var material = new BABYLON.StandardMaterial("myFirstMaterial", scene);
sphere.material = material;
```

Important properties of a material taking a BABYLON.Color3:

- material.diffuseColor
- material.specularColor
- material.emissiveColor
- material.ambientColor

Important properties of a material taking a BABYLON.Texture:

- material.diffuseTexture
- material.emissiveTexture
- material.ambientTexture
- material.opacityTexture
- material.specularTexture
- material.bumpTexture
- material.reflectionTexture

A reflection texture must have its coordinate mode set in order to be displayed.

Use FresnelsParameters to display some transparency on a mesh:

```
material.diffuseFresnelParameters = new BABYLON.FresnelParameters();
material.opacityFresnelParameters = new BABYLON.FresnelParameters();
material.reflectionFresnelParameters = new BABYLON.FresnelParameters();
material.emissiveFresnelParameters = new BABYLON.FresnelParameters();
```

Create shadows with a ShadowGenerator and a DirectionalLight:

```
var dl = new BABYLON.DirectionalLight("dir", new BABYLON.Vector3(1,-1,-0.5),
scene);
dl.position = new BABYLON.Vector3(0, 40, 0);
var shadows = new BABYLON.ShadowGenerator(1024, dl);
```

To receive shadows:

```
mesh.receiveShadows = true;
```

To cast shadows:

```
shadows.getShadowMap().renderList.push(mesh);
```

Multi-materials:

```
var multimat = new BABYLON.MultiMaterial("multimat", scene);
multimat.subMaterials.push(standardmat1);
multimat.subMaterials.push(standardmat2);
multimat.subMaterials.push(standardmat3);
```

Create a sub-mesh:

```
cube.subMeshes = [];
var submesh1 = new BABYLON.SubMesh(0, vertexStart, vertexCount, indiceStart,
indiceCount, mesh);
cube.subMeshes.push(submesh1);
```

CHAPTER 6 - EXPORTERS

As you've seen in the previous chapter, creating standard geometries that you can use in your scene is very easy. But even if you can create awesome games only with primitives (think Super Hexagon, Tetris...), a vast majority of games and applications need more complex objects. These external 3D models are created by a professional with a dedicated tool: 3DS Max, Blender, Maya...

In this chapter, the following topics will be explained:

- How to download and install the *3DS max* Babylon.js plugin;

- How to download and install the *Unity3D* Babylon.js plugin;

- How to download and install the *Blender* Babylon.js plugin;

- How to use these plugins to export a complex model or a complete scene;

- How to check your work by using an external web application.

Installing the 3DS Max plugin

The plugin is designed for 3DS Max 2013 and 2015. To download it, go to the Github project (https://github.com/BabylonJS/Babylon.js), click on the folder *Exporters*, then on the folder *3ds Max*.

In this folder, you can find the source code of the exporter if you want to update it, and a zip file *Max2Babylon-XX.zip* (where XX is the exporter version, currently 0.6.0).
Click on the zip file, and click on the *Download* button.

Extract the content of the zip file on your computer, and open the directory corresponding to your 3DS Max version.
By default, Windows blocks all .dll files coming from the web, so we have to unblock them first. Select the first .dll file, and with a right click select *Properties*, click on the button *Unblock*, and then *OK*.

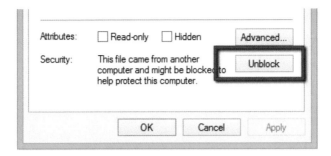

Repeat this process for all .dll files. Finally, make sure 3ds Max is not running, and move all .dll files into the installation directory of 3DS Max (in C:/Programs/Autodesk/3ds Max 2015/bin/assemblies).
The next time you will start 3ds Max, the plugin will be automatically launched, and a new tab should appear:

Congratulations! You did it ☺

Features

Scene properties

If you right-click on your scene, you will have a menu *Babylon -> Babylon Properties:*

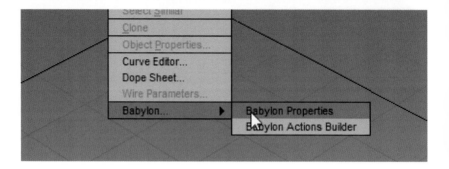

The scene properties allow you to do two things:

- Set the scene **gravity**

- **Export quaternions for all nodes instead of Euler angles**.

It's important to notice this last option is selected by default. If this option is selected, an exported model rotation won't be updated by setting its **rotation** parameter. Instead, you will have to use the **rotationQuaternion** parameter.

You surely noticed the submenu Babylon Actions Builder. This submenu will be used to register actions between objects, but is not yet finished at the time of the writing.

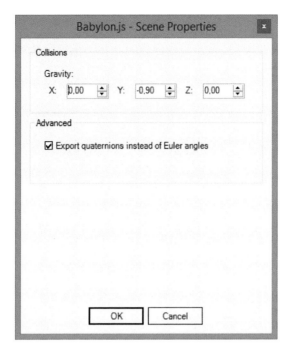

Object properties

With a right click on a mesh, select the menu *Babylon -> Babylon Properties* to open the window Object Properties:

With this window, you can set the following properties:

- **Check collisions**: Activate it to enable collisions between the camera and this object. False by default.

- **Do not export**: Self-explanatory, this object won't be exported. False by default.

- **Pickable**: This object can be picked with the mouse. False by default.

- **Try to optimize vertices**: The Babylon exporter will try to optimize the number of vertices to export instead of exporting everything naively (if a vertex is part of two faces, this vertex won't be exported twice with this option checked). False by default.

- **Show bounding box**: Display the bounding box of this object in the scene. False by default.

- **Show submeshes bounding boxes**. Same as above. False by default.

- **Alpha index**: Used to sort transparent meshes. The mesh with the bigger alpha index is rendered first (then the depth is taken into account). Default value is 1000.

- **Auto animate**: All animations for this object will start when this object is being added to the scene. True by default.

- **From/To/Loop**: The starting and ending frame for this object, and if the animation loops. Default values are 0, 100 and true.

- **Impostor**: Add an impostor to this object. Default is none.

- **Mass/Friction/Restitution**: set the physics value of the impostor. Default values are 0.20, 0.20, and 0.20.

Light properties

If you create a standard light and right click on it, select the menu Babylon -> Babylon Properties to display this window:

The options **Do not export**, and **animations** are exactly the same as the Object properties window.

Camera properties

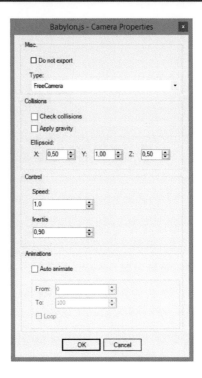

In this window, you can choose the kind of camera you want to create in Babylon.js. You can also:

- **Check collision**: The camera can collide against objects where check collisions is activated.

- **Apply gravity**: The camera will be subject to the scene's gravity (in the Scene properties window)

- **Ellipsoid**: With collisions enabled, the camera will be wrapped in an ellipsoid, the size of which can be set here.

- **Speed / inertia**: The speed and inertia of the camera. Default values are 1 and 0.9.

- **Animations**: Same as in Object properties window.

The exporter window

When your scene is ready to be exported, click on the **Babylon** tab on the top menu, and click on **Babylon File Exporter** to display the exporter window.

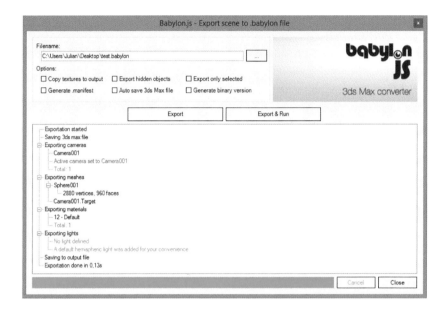

This window is composed of 3 panels:

- A top panel with a file path and a button. With this panel, you choose where your Babylon file will be exported by clicking on the right button.
- Several options and two buttons Export and Export & Run
- A log panel

The Export button should be used to create the Babylon file representing your scene. The Export & Run button will also create the Babylon file, but will also launch your default browser and run the newly made Babylon file. This button is very useful if you just want to test the render of your scene in Babylon.js.

As babylon.js script is retrieved directly from the official website directly, you should have internet access in order to correctly use Export & Run.

The log panel indicates in real time which mesh has been exported, which material, and if there are any problems with these objects.

What you should know

Camera

If you want to test your scene right away by using the button Export & Run, your scene should have a camera created. Otherwise, the log panel will display the warning "No camera defined".
If you have more than one camera, the first one will be set as activeCamera in Babylon.

Light

If you don't have any lights in your scene, the exporter will add a hemispheric light by default. The log panel will display the warning "No light defined – A default hemispheric light was added for your convenience".

Pivot and position

The object position will be defined with your object pivot position. In the image below, the pivot position is not at the center of the box: updating the object position in Babylon.js will update this pivot position, and not the box position.

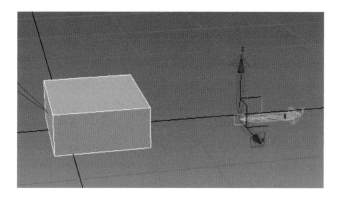

Figure 37 - Position and pivot point

Negative scale

Using a negative scale will reverse the normal of your objects. These objects will appear correctly in 3DSMax, but incorrectly in a Babylon.js application.

Texture transparency

Babylon supports PNG, DDS and TGA formats for texture transparency. You can choose to include the transparency directly in your diffuse texture, or create an opacity map. Here are the options to check if you want to have transparency on your diffuse texture:

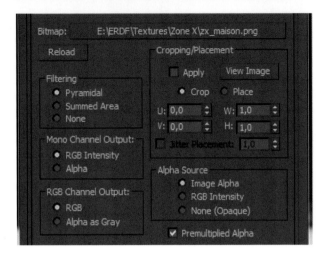

Now that you know all about the exporter features, it's time to use it!

Using the exporter

First, create the model you will be using in the Key class. I choose to create a simple key (you might recognize a little inspiration from the Zelda games).

As you can see, the key has 3 key frames creating a floating animation. Its material has no diffuse color (set to black), but a self-illumination color (corresponding to the emissive color in Babylon.js).

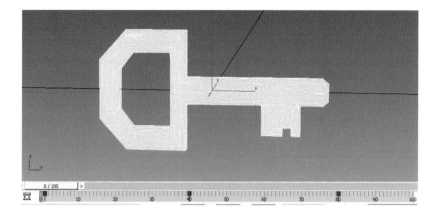

Figure 38 - The key!

The only thing left to do is to export this key as a Babylon file, and we're done with 3DS Max. As the animation is going from frame 0 to frame 80, the Babylon properties for this file have to be updated. And we're done!

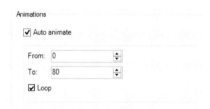

Installing the Unity3D plugin

Since version 2.1, it is possible to create your scene with Unity3D 5 and export it in Babylon.js with a custom exporter, created by David Rousset and David Catuhe.

Its installation is very easy: clone the repository or download the whole zip file on Github:

HTTPS clone URL

https://github.com/t

You can clone with HTTPS, SSH, or Subversion. ☉

Clone in Desktop

Download ZIP

Unzip the archive if you have to, and navigate to the folder *Exporters -> Unity 5*.

Every Unity project has a folder called *Assets*: you just have to copy the whole folder *Unity3D2Babylon* into the *Assets* folder of your Unity project, and you're done! Unity will automatically compile your project, and magically add a new menu entry called BabylonJS, as shown in the screenshot below:

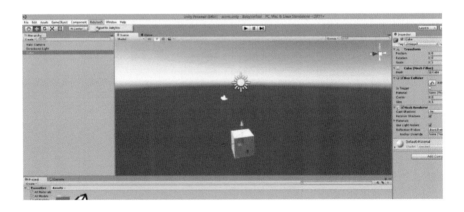

Using the Unity exporter

In this scene, there is only a default cube (menu *GameObject -> 3D Object -> Cube*), attached to a looping rotation animation.

When clicking on the menu BabylonJS -> Export to .babylon, a small popup appears:

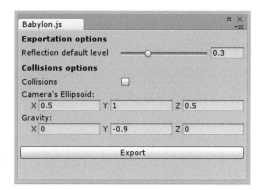

Let's explain the exporter's parameters:

- Reflection default level: the texture level
- Collisions: check this if you want to enable collisions between your camera and meshes (will set scene.collisionsEnabled to true)
- Camera ellipsoid: The ellipsoid around the camera that will raise collisions.
- Gravity: the scene gravity.

Once all parameters are chosen, you can click on "Export" to create a .babylon file. This file will have the same name as the Unity scene.

That's it! Easy right? With its integrated drag and drop playground, Unity can be easily used to import your meshes and create your scene, while doing all the game logic with Babylon.js.

Last thing: all animations linked to position, rotation and scaling of meshes can be exported too! If you want to check if a specific feature can be exported or not, you will find an exhaustive list in the official documentation.

Installing the Blender plugin

As with the Unity plugin, you have first to clone the Babylon.js repository, or download it as a zip file from Github.
Open Blender, and select the menu File -> User Preferences...

Navigate to the tab "Add-ons" and click on the button "Install from File..." at the bottom of the popup window:

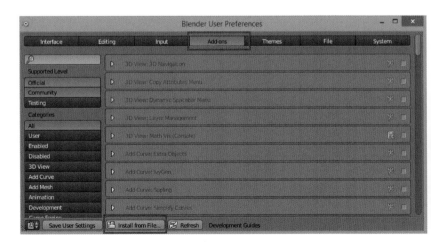

Browse your hard drive to where you stored the Babylon.js repository, and select the file Exporters/Blender/io_export_blender.py:

Click on the button "Install from File..." to install the plugin. Finally, navigate to the tab Import-Export, and activate the plugin by clicking on the small checkbox:

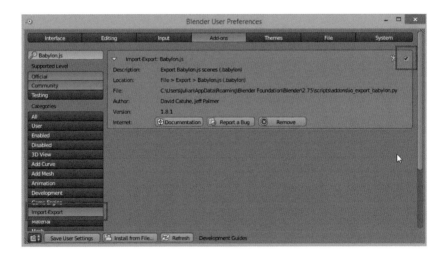

You will find the exporter in the menu File -> Export:

Using the Blender exporter

By clicking on this menu entry, you will export your scene in a .babylon format. With every export, a log file is generated in the same folder as your Babylon scene: do not hesitate to share this log file if any problems occur during the export.

A lot of features are supported through the Blender plugin, you can consult an exhaustive list in the official documentation here.

Check your work with the sandbox

The sandbox is a web application available at http://www.babylonjs.com/sandbox/where you can drag and drop a Babylon file from your hard drive to visualize it. It can be used to test your assets without having to set up a small application.

CHAPTER 7 - READING AND USING A BABYLON FILE

After successfully exporting your custom model (or your custom scene), we should be able to load it in our game. In this chapter, we will first explain how to enable offline support for a Babylon.js application with manifest files. Then, you will learn 3 different ways to load a .babylon file (scene and/or model).

Enable offline support

If you want to create web applications that can work both online and offline, you have to find a way to persistently store data inside a user browser. Such a way exists through the Indexed Database API (or IndexedDB): it's a local database available within the client browser where you can store and retrieve data with a key.

When you deal with custom 3D models and textures, this data can only be used from a web server. However, if they are stored in the IndexedDB of the browser, they can be retrieved while the user is offline.

Babylon.js provides a way to easily deal with the IndexedDB of your browser and thus enable offline support: a .manifest file.

A .manifest file is a simple piece of JSON composed of 3 keys:

```
{
  "version" : 1,
  "enableSceneOffline" : true,
  "enableTexturesOffline" : true
}
```

When a .babylon file is loaded by the framework, the first thing it will try to locate is the manifest file corresponding to the given model. If this manifest is not found (404 error), Babylon will load the model. If the manifest is found, its values are loaded:

- **version** is the current version of your model. Incrementing this value will make the framework reload your scene and store it again in the database.

- **enableSceneOffline** set to true will enable offline support for this model.

- **enableTexturesOffline** set to true will store all textures of your model as a Blob in the IndexedDB.

To be found by the framework, a manifest file should have the same name as the .babylon file (followed by .manifest), and in the same directory as your assets. Example:

Scene: myCustomModel**.babylon**
Manifest: myCustomModel**.babylon.manifest**

Read a Babylon file

There are 3 ways to read a Babylon file. Let's describe it from the simplest to the more elaborate.

Just notice that **all textures linked to your model should be in the same folder as your Babylon file.**

Import a mesh

The first way to import a mesh in a Babylon scene is to use the method BABYLON.SceneLoader.ImportMesh. This method imports all meshes, materials and particle systems found in the Babylon file.

It takes a filename and a Babylon scene already created, imports the specified meshes, and gives control back to the developer with a method containing all loaded meshes (useful if you want to update the meshes' position, materials, or whatever you need changed). Here is the method prototype:

```
BABYLON.SceneLoader.ImportMesh(meshName, folderName, fileName, scene,
onSuccess, onProgress, onError);
```

Let's explain all these parameters:
- meshName: The name of the mesh you want to import. This name has been set in the 3D modeller. If your Babylon file has several meshes, just put an empty string "".
- folderName: The folder where the Babylon file is stored. Don't forget the ending slash '/'
- fileName: The Babylon file name.
- scene: The Babylon Scene object.
- onSuccess: a callback function called when the mesh has been loaded. Takes three parameters: meshes, particle systems corresponding to the loaded objects, and loaded skeletons (see the section CHAPTER 12 – Skeletons and bones system)

Importing a mesh is an asynchronous process (via XHR request). This means you don't know when the mesh will be loaded! For example, the following code:

```
console.log("toto");
BABYLON.SceneLoader.ImportMesh(meshName, folderName, fileName, scene,
function(meshes, ps) {
  console.log("loaded");
```

```
});
console.log("titi");
```

Will produce the following output:

```
toto
titi
loaded
```

That means you cannot use an imported mesh outside the callback function!
- onProgress: callback function used to get the loading progress of your babylon file. Takes X parameters.
- onError: callback function called when an error occurs.

Load a scene

The second way to import a Babylon file is to use the method BABYLON.SceneLoader.Load. This function takes only the references to a Babylon file, the Babylon engine, and creates a new scene.
The method prototype is the following:

```
BABYLON.SceneLoader.Load(folderName, fileName, engine, onSuccess, onProgress, onError)
```

Parameters are:
- folderName: The folder where the Babylon file is stored. Don't forget the ending slash '/'
- fileName: The Babylon file name.
- engine: The Babylon engine used to create the scene.
- onSuccess: same as above.
- onProgress: same as above.
- onError: same as above.

This method should be used if you want to create a totally new scene from the specified file.

Using the Assets Manager

A third way to load a Babylon file is to use the Assets Manager. The Assets Manager is an awesome tool you can use to load all kind of files: images, text files, binary files, and mesh files (aka .babylon files).

It will automatically create a loading screen (that you can customize if needed) and load all files you specified.

We will use this method to load all our external assets by doing the following:
- Create the assets manager
- Load all assets
- Store these assets in memory (in an array)
- Create the game.

Using the AssetsManager is easy. You can create it like this:

```
var loader = new BABYLON.AssetsManager(scene);
```

Then you can add your mesh tasks like this:

```
var task = loader.addMeshTask(name, meshName, folderName, fileName);
```

The name corresponds to the task name. meshName, folderName and filename are relative to the Babylon file.

You can set a callback function when the loading succeeds or fails:

```
task.onSuccess = function(t) {...}
task.onError = function(t) {...}
```

Finally, you can set a callback function to the loader when all tasks are loaded:

```
loader.onFinish = function () {...}
```

Everything is greatly described in the official Babylon documentation (http://doc.babylonjs.com/tutorials/How_to_use_AssetsManager).

Back to the game

Let's define an array in our Game class that will contain all our 3D external assets and their animations:

```
// Contains all 3D models
this.assets = [];
```

The asset manager is created in the Game constructor, and the loading screen background color is slightly updated:

```
// Creates a loader
var loader = new BABYLON.AssetsManager(this.scene);
loader.loadingUIBackgroundColor = "#2c2b29";
```

We should now define a data structure to handle all our 3D models. Of course, we could have added all our tasks "as is", but isn't our goal to create beautiful code?

```
// The Key animation
var animsKey = [];
animsKey["idle"] = {from:0, to:80, speed:1, loop:true};

// All models to load
var toLoad = [
  {
    name:"key",
```

```
  folder:"assets/",
  filename:"key.babylon",
  anims : animsKey
 }
];
```

The object **toLoad** will contain all our 3D assets, with its filename, its folder and animations if any are present.

We can now create a loading task for each asset:

```
var _this = this;
// For each object to load
toLoad.forEach(function(tl) {

  var task = loader.addMeshTask(tl.name, "", tl.folder, tl.filename);
  task.onSuccess = function(t) {
  // Set all mesh invisible
  t.loadedMeshes.forEach(function(mesh) {
    mesh.isVisible = false;
  });
  // Save it in the asset array
  _this.assets[t.name] = {meshes:t.loadedMeshes, anims:tl.anims};
  };
});
```

This block of code can be read like this: for all objects to load, add a mesh task to the loader. When this asset has been correctly loaded, all meshes composing this asset are set to be invisible. Finally, the asset is stored in the assets folder of the Game class with the task name as the array key.

Running the index.html page will show you a loading screen, but our game didn't change. We should now update the Key class, to replace the donuts with our beautiful key.

In the Key constructor, just replace the line where the torus is created by this line:

```
var key = game.assets['key'].meshes[0].clone();
key.isVisible = true;
```

game.assets['key'].meshes[0] retrieves the first mesh of the key asset. As our model is only composed of one mesh, it's perfect ☺. The mesh is then cloned, in order to create several geometries of the same asset. Finally, the key is set to visible.

And tadaaa!

The key is not animated here, we will see how to create animations in the very next chapter. In the meanwhile, are you ready for a little exercise?

Exercise

Replace the primitives created for the Apple class and the Spike class in the chapter 2 with the Babylon assets provided with this book. The spike mesh has an animation from the frame 0 to frame 100.

Here is what you should see after this exercise:

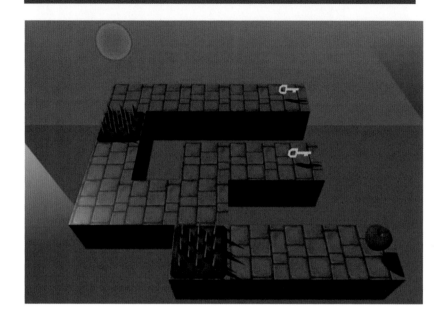

CHEAT SHEET

Create a manifest file to allow the storage of your meshes in the browser IndexedDB. The file should have the same name as your Babylon file and be in the same folder:

  ➢ scene_name.babylon
  ➢ scene_name.babylon.manifest

Import a Babylon file into an existing scene:

```
BABYLON.SceneLoader.ImportMesh(meshName, folderName, fileName, scene,
onSuccess, onProgress, onError);
```

Import a Babylon file by creating a new scene:

```
BABYLON.SceneLoader.Load(folderName, fileName, engine, onSuccess,
onProgress, onError)
```

Using the Assets Manager to load external resources:

```
var loader =  new BABYLON.AssetsManager(scene);
var task = loader.addMeshTask(name, meshName, folderName, fileName);
task.onSuccess = function(t) {...}
task.onError = function(t) {...}
loader.onFinish = function () {...}
```

CHAPTER 8 - ANIMATIONS

In this chapter, we will see how to add some life to our objects by giving them animations. In Babylon.js, there are several ways to create animations:

- A simple way, where the developer only has to specify a starting state and an ending state, and the system interpolates everything by itself.

- A more complex way, where the developer is in charge of everything.

- A design way, where everything is handled in a 3D modeler with key frames.

Create an animation

Creating a new Animation object is the simplest way to give dynamics to your objects. It works by giving several values to specific parameters according to key frames: every key represents the value of the parameter for a key frame.

You can animate any property you desire for a given object, but this property must be of the following type:

- Number
- BABYLON.Vector2
- BABYLON.Vector3
- BABYLON.Color3
- BABYLON.Quaternion
- BABYLON.Matrix

For each of these types, a method giving the interpolation between two values is provided.

First, you have to create a new Animation object:

```
var animationBox = new BABYLON.Animation(name, targetProperty,
framePerSecond, dataType, loopMode)
```

Parameters are:

- name : The animation name
- targetProperty: The object property you want to animate. It's a string that can contain dots, like scaling.x, or material.diffuseColor.r.
- framePerSecond: The number of frames per second this animation should be running.
- dataType: The type of property you want to update (defined above).
- loopMode: The loop mode of the animation. Can be set to the following values:

  - BABYLON.Animation.ANIMATIONLOOPMODE_RELATIVE: The last values are kept to restart the animation. Runs the animation in a loop.

  - BABYLON.Animation.ANIMATIONLOOPMODE_CYCLE: The animation is restarted from scratch. Runs the animation in a loop.

  - BABYLON.Animation.ANIMATIONLOOPMODE_CONSTANT: The animation is stopped when it finishes.

Let's create an animation for our apple: we want it to levitate up and down just above the ground:

```
var animationBox = new BABYLON.Animation("appleAnim", "position.y", 30,
BABYLON.Animation.ANIMATIONTYPE_FLOAT,
BABYLON.Animation.ANIMATIONLOOPMODE_CYCLE);
```

Our animation will run in a loop, and will update the y position of our mesh.

Then, 3 key frames must be set:

```
// Animation keys
var keys = [{
  frame: 0,
  value: 1
},{
  frame: 30,
  value: 1.5
},{
  frame: 60,
  value: 1
}];
animationBox.setKeys(keys);
```

At frame 0, the y position of the mesh will be 1. At frame 30 it will be 1.5, and it will be back to 1 at frame 60: our animation will run from frame 0 to frame 60 at 30 frames per second.

Finally, link the animation to our mesh, and start the animation:

```
this.animations.push(animationBox);
scene.beginAnimation(this, 0, 60, true, 1.0);
```

scene.beginAnimation takes as the first parameter the mesh to animate, the starting frame and the ending frame. The next parameter should be set to true if the animation loops, and the last parameter is the speed ratio.

If you run your game now, you should see your apple going up and down in the air. Cool isn't it?

The method beginAnimation returns an instance of the class BABYLON.Animatable. This object has several interesting properties:

fromFrame	The starting frame of this animation
toFrame	The ending frame of this animation
loopAnimation	True if the animation loops, false otherwise
speedRatio	The speed ratio of the animation
onAnimationEnd	Function called when the animation ends.
pause()	Suspend the animation
restart()	Reset the animation
stop()	Stop the animation

A more complex way to animate an object

A Babylon scene object provides two methods to control exactly what your object should do in each frame:

```
scene.registerBeforeRunder(function() {
  // ...
});
scene.registerAfterRunder(function() {
  // ...
});
```

The given function will be called before (or after) the frame creation.
Be careful of what you put in this function, as it will be called 60 times per second.

Retrieve an animation created in an external tool

The key frames discussed in the previous chapter can also be created in a 3D modeling tool such as 3DS Max or Blender. In this case, all key frames are in the Babylon file of the asset.

Once your file has been imported, you just have to start the animation from the starting frame to the end frame, and you're done!

Here is an example for the Key class, where animations frames have been stored in an array:

```
var keyAnims = game.assets['key'].anims['idle'];
this.getScene().beginAnimation(key, keyAnims.from, keyAnims.to, keyAnims.loop, keyAnims.speed);
```

By retrieving the Animatable object returned by beginAnimation, you can control the animation as you want.

Now, it's time to take control of the player and make him move on the level!

CHEAT SHEET

Create an animation:

```
var animationBox = new BABYLON.Animation(name, targetProperty,
framePerSecond, dataType, loopMode);
```

name :   string ⇨ the animation name

targetProperty: string ⇨ the property you want to animate

framePerSecond: number ⇨ the number of frames per second
                            this animation will run at.

dataType: number ⇨ the type of data relative to the
targetProperty

loopMode: number ⇨ The kind of loop (restart the
                            animation, keep last values, ...)

Set keys to an animation:

```
var keys = [{frame : ??, value : ??}, ...];
animationBox.setKeys(keys);
```

Start an animation:

```
scene.beginAnimation(node, startFrame, endFrame, loop, speed);
```

node: BABYLON.Node ⇨ the object to animate

startFrame: number ⇨ the starting frame of the
animation

endFrame: number ⇨ the ending frame of the animation

loop: boolean ⇨ true if the animation should loop,
                            false otherwise.

CHAPTER 9 - USER INPUTS

Now that we have built a good-looking environment, we have to make the game react to the player inputs. We will take a look at how to add controls to our ball: first the ball will react to the keyboard, then we will learn how to use a gamepad with Babylon.js.

What we would like

By pressing the right and left arrow keys, the ball will rotate. Up and down arrows will make the ball move forward or backwards.

Make the player move like Jagger

The first easy solution you can think about is to link the keydown event (fired by the browser) to the ball.
Let's try it with the Player class:

```
var _this = this;
window.addEventListener("keydown", function(e) {
  switch (e.keyCode) {
    case 39: // right
      _this.rotation.y += 1;
      break;
    case 37: // left
      _this.rotation.y -= 1;
      break;
    case 38://bot:
      _this.position.z += 1;
      break;
```

```
case 40://top:
  _this.position.z -= 1;
  break;
}
});
```

But two problems appear:

- The rotation and the movement are not smooth
- The ball is not moving forward, but along the global Z axis.

Indeed, the first problem is caused by the delay between two keydown events. This delay is approximately 250 ms, so by keeping the key pressed the player position and rotation will be updated to a maximum of every 0.25 second. Not so great...

The second problem is because of our code: in this example, the global z-axis is used, whereas it's the local z-axis that should be used.

The first issue can be solved pretty easily by calling using the method registerBeforeRender. This special method can be used on the BABYLON.Scene object and BABYLON.Mesh object, and registers a function to be called just before the render loop.

Note that the functions unregisterBeforeRender, registerAfterRender, and unregisterAfterRender also exists.

The keydown event will then enable a boolean giving the direction of the rotation (or the position), and our special function will check this boolean 60 times per second, and move accordingly. The code should be now:

```
// Two boolean giving the direction (forward/backward)
this.directions = [0,0];
// Two boolean giving the rotation (right/left)
```

```
this.rotations = [0,0];

var _this = this;
this.getScene().registerBeforeRender(function() {
  // Move the player is possible
  _this.move();
  //...
});
```

The event listener:

```
window.addEventListener("keydown", function(e) {
  switch (e.keyCode) {
    case 39: // right
    _this.rotations[0] = 1;
    break;
    case 37: // left
    _this.rotations[1] = 1;
    break;
    case 38://bot:
    _this.directions[0] = 1;
    break;
    case 40://top:
    _this.directions[1] = 1;
    break;
  }
});
window.addEventListener("keyup", function(e) {
  switch (e.keyCode) {
    case 39: // right
    case 37: // left
    _this.rotations = [0,0];
    break;
    case 38://bot:
    case 40://top:
    _this.directions = [0,0];
    break;
  }
});
```

And the move function:

```
Player.prototype.move = function() {
  if (this.directions[0] != 0) {
```

```
  this._moveTo(-1);
  }
  if (this.directions[1] != 0) {
    this._moveTo(1);
  }
  if (this.rotations[0]  != 0) {
    this._rotateTo(0.05);
  }
  if (this.rotations[1]  != 0) {
    this._rotateTo(-0.05);
  }
};
```

Our first problem is now solved!

For the second problem, we have to transform the global Z-axis into the player's local system in order to use the local Z-axis. To convert to convert world coordinates to local coordinates, we need the world matrix of the local system (our player). This local system can be accessed with the method **getWorldMatrix**.

Do you remember the local system we described in Chapter 1 (World space and local space)? That's right, it's the world matrix we are talking about.

The code of the function **_moveTo** is just below:

```
Player.prototype._moveTo = function(s) {
  // Compute the world matrix of the player
  this.computeWorldMatrix();
  // Moving forward along the global z-axis
  var v = new BABYLON.Vector3(0,0,s);
  // Get the world matrix
  var m = this.getWorldMatrix();
  // Transform the global vector into local vector
  var v2 = BABYLON.Vector3.TransformCoordinates(v, m);
  v2.subtractInPlace(this.position);
  v2.normalize().scaleInPlace(0.05);
  // Add this new vector to the player position
  this.position.addInPlace(v2);
};
```

The method **BABYLON.Vector3.TransformCoordinates** is used to transform the given vector into the given space (the second parameter – the world matrix of the player).

Now your player should move and rotate smoothly by pressing the arrow keys of your keyboard.

Control the player with a gamepad

The Gamepad API allows you to interact with your browser using a game pad, without the need of a specific driver. Any modern gamepad supported by your system should be detected and usable.

> At the time of writing, Internet Explorer 11 doesn't support the Gamepad API.

Babylon.js provides several classes about this Gamepad API that eases the process of mapping each button to an action.

The class **BABYLON.Gamepads** is the Gamepad manager class. Its constructor takes a function called when a gamepad is connected to your browser. As this function will be called for each gamepad connected to your computer, creating a new instance of class Gamepads should not be called in your Player class, but in your Game class.
The **_initGame** method is now:

```
Game.prototype._initGame = function() {
  var _this = this;
  var onGamepadConnected = function(g) {
    // A gamepad is connected, the player and the level are created
    _this.player = new Player(_this, g);
    _this.shadows.getShadowMap().renderList.push(_this.player);
```

```
_this.scene.activeCamera.target = _this.player;

_this.level = Level.FromInts(levels[_this.currentLevel], _this);
_this.player.position = _this.level.start.position.clone();
_this.player.position.y = 1;
};

// Listen to connected gamepads.
new BABYLON.Gamepads(onGamepadConnected);
};
```

The Player class now takes the connected gamepad as a constructor parameter, where the gamepad configuration will be done.

Two kind of gamepads

Babylon.js provides two classes to map actions to the gamepad buttons: BABYLON.GenericPad and BABYLON.Xbox360Pad.

A generic pad is composed of two joysticks and a set of buttons (composed of the directional arrows and all buttons on the pad, triggers included), whereas all buttons are identified for the Xbox pad: it is composed of two joysticks, a directional arrow and a set of buttons (A, B, X, Y, start, select, LB, LT, RB, RT).

Here are the functions you can use on both classes:

onbuttondown	Takes a function as a parameter. The callback function is called with the button code when a button is down.
onbuttonup	Takes a function as a parameter. The callback function is called with the button code when a button is up.

Here are the functions relative to the Xbox360 pad:

onlefttriggerchanged onrighttriggerchanged	Takes a function as a parameter. The callback function is called when the left/right trigger (LT/RT button) is changed, the updated value is sent as parameter.
ondpaddown ondpadup	Takes a function as a parameter. The callback function is called with the button code when the directional pad is down/up.

Let's use these functions to make our game work with a XBOX controller.

First, we have to adapt our Player class to make it work with a Gamepad object. Here is the new method Game.initGame:

```
Game.prototype._initGame = function() {
  var _this = this;
  var onGamepadConnected = function(g) {
    // A gamepad is connected, the player and the level are created
    _this.player = new Player(_this, g);
    _this.shadows.getShadowMap().renderList.push(_this.player);
    _this.scene.activeCamera.target = _this.player;

    _this.level = Level.FromInts(levels[_this.currentLevel], _this);
    _this.player.position = _this.level.start.position.clone();
    _this.player.position.y = 1;
  };

  // Listen to connected gamepads.
  var gps = new BABYLON.Gamepads(onGamepadConnected);
  gps._startMonitoringGamepads();

};
```

You can see a new object BABYLON.Gamepads is created.

In the Player class, we have to configure this gamepad:

```
Player.prototype._configureGamepad = function(gp) {
  gp.ondpaddown(function (b) {
    switch(b) {
      case 0: // UP
        _this.directions[0] = 1;
        break;
```

```
      case 1: // DOWN
        _this.directions[1] = 1;
        break;
      case 2: // LEFT
        _this.rotations[1] = 1;
        break;
      case 3: // RIGHT
        _this.rotations[0] = 1;
        break;
    }
  });
  gp.ondpadup(function (b) {
    switch(b) {
      case 0: // UP
      case 1: // DOWN
        _this.directions = [0,0];
        break;
      case 2: // LEFT
      case 3: // RIGHT
        _this.rotations = [0,0];
        break;
    }
  });
};
```

And that's all! All the hard work to check the gamepad value is directly done in Babylon.js.

You are now able to control your ball, but the player is not falling off the level. It's time to rectify this by using a physics engine to simulate the gravity and collisions.

CHAPTER 10 - USING A PHYSICS ENGINE

In this chapter, we will see how to use a basic physics engine integrated with Babylon.js called Oimo.js. Oimo.js is a JavaScript conversion, which was made by a French guy named Lo-th, of OimoPhysics, a physics engine written in ActionScript.

Oimo.js is the Babylon.js default physics engine, but cannon.js is also supported and integrated, and can be used if needed.
This physics engine provides a simulation of gravity, and collisions between rigid bodies. We will see how to activate the engine and how to set rigid bodies to our game components.

Enable the physics engine

The first thing we need to do is to add the library to our project. Navigate to the Babylon.js main repository on Github, download the file Oimo.js and add it in our lib folder. Don't forget to add the corresponding line in index.html:

```
<script src="lib/OIMO.js"></script>
```

Next step: enable the engine! Add this line in the method _initScene of the Game class:

```
scene.enablePhysics(new BABYLON.Vector3(0,-9,0), new
BABYLON.OimoJSPlugin());
```

And that's all! You will enable the physics engine with two parameters:
- The gravity is set to (0, -9.8, 0)
- The physics engine used is Oimo.js

But you could have done something like this in order to double the gravity used in your game:

```
scene.enablePhysics(new BABYLON.Vector3(0, -20, 0), new
BABYLON.OimoJSPlugin());
```

As said above, the plugin BABYLON.CannonJSPlugin exists for cannon.js.

Using impostors

A physics engine works by adding a rigid body to a mesh. Every mesh that have a rigid body will interact in the physics world.

This rigid body can have three kind of shapes in Oimo.js (also called impostors):
- Box impostor
- Plane impostor
- Sphere impostor

These impostors are simple shapes used to approximate heavy physics calculations. All collisions will be performed on the impostor, not on the original mesh. Thus, it won't be possible to have pixel perfect collisions (unless your mesh is a box, then it's awesome).

To set an impostor to a game component, use the method setPhysicsState:

```
var body = mesh.setPhysicsState(BABYLON.PhysicsEngine.BoxImpostor, {mass:0,
restitution : 0.5, friction:0.5});
```

This method takes two parameters:

- The impostor to use (BoxImpostor, PlaneImpostor or SphereImpostor);
- An object representing the physics material.

The physics material is composed of 3 attributes:

- A mass
- A friction coefficient
- A restitution coefficient

The mass is self-explanatory. If set to 0, the object won't be affected by the world gravity, and thus won't move at all. The default value is 0.

The friction coefficient represents the resistance when two objects are sliding against each other. 0 means no friction, and 1 means a lot of friction. Its default value is 0.2.

The restitution coefficient represents the bounciness of the material. It's a value between 0 and 1, with 0 representing no bounciness at all. The default value is 0.2.

The returned object is an instance of the rigid body used by the physics engine the game is using. Here with Oimo.js, this object is an instance of Oimo.Body.

Impulse

Once the mesh has its physic body, it is not possible to move it by updating its position/rotation. Indeed, the object position and rotation is inherently linked to the physics body position and rotation. To move an object, two solutions exists:

- Move the physics body

- Apply an impulse to the body

Apply an impulse means to apply a force in a direction on a point in the local space of the object. The corresponding method is:

```
mesh.applyImpulse(force, position);
```

Parameters **force** and **position** are two instances of **BABYLON.Vector3**.

Apply impostors on our game components

Let's add a physics state to the Block class:

```
this.setPhysicsState(BABYLON.PhysicsEngine.BoxImpostor, {mass:0, restitution : 0.5, friction:0.5});
```

Our blocks won't fall (their mass is 0), and they have a medium restitution and friction coefficient. Our player should also have an impostor:

```
this.body = this.setPhysicsState(BABYLON.PhysicsEngine.BoxImpostor, {mass:1, friction:0.9});
```

In order to move our player, we will generate an impulse following the local Z-axis. Instead of updating the player position, do this:

```
this.applyImpulse(v2, this.position);
```

Where **v2** is the force direction, and **this.position** is the player position.

Rotations

When a physics engine is used and an impostor is applied on a mesh, updating the rotation attribute has no effect on the mesh, for the same reason as described in the section on impulse. Here, we will update the physics body by using quaternions.

Quaternions

A Quaternion is a mathematical way to represent a rotation. It is commonly represented by a vector with 4 dimensions (x, y, z, w). They answer a lot of problems developers can have with Euler rotations (Gimbal lock for example), and they can be easily manipulated. The fun thing is they can be combined, and it magically (well, sort of) works, whereas combining multiple Euler rotations almost never works the way you want it to.

Babylon.js provides an implementation of quaternions with several methods to help the developer to use them. The basic operation is the multiply method: it is used to add several rotations.

```
var q = new BABYLON.Quaternion();
var q2 = new BABYLON.Quaternion();
var newRotation = q.multiply(q2);
```

Another interesting method is RotationYawPitchRoll: this method takes 3 parameters and returns the quaternion corresponding of 3 rotations: yaw along the Y-axis, pitch along the X-axis, and roll along the Z-axis:

```
var q = BABYLON.Quaternion.RotationYawPitchRoll(Math.PI/2, 0, 0);
```

You also have the method RotationAxis that gives you the quaternion corresponding to the given rotation around the given axis:

```
var rotationQ = BABYLON.Quaternion.RotationAxis(BABYLON.Axis.Z, Math.PI/2);
```

We will use the attribute rotationQuaternion of our mesh to rotate it.

Be careful, when rotationQuaternion is not null, rotation is not taken into account!

The _rotateTo method of the Player class is then:

```
Player.prototype._rotateTo = function(s) {
// get Mesh quaternion
var mq = this.rotationQuaternion;
var q = BABYLON.Quaternion.RotationAxis(BABYLON.Axis.Y, s);
this.rotationQuaternion = q.multiply(mq);
this.body.body.setQuaternion(this.rotationQuaternion);
this.body.body.sleeping = false;
};
```

The method setQuaternion (which name is explanatory) is used on the physics body to update the mesh rotation. Finally, the attribute sleeping is set to false to be aware of transformations. If this line is not set, the physics body won't move after few seconds.

Exercise

Try to update the values of the physics material of the player and of the ground. Update the restitution coefficient and see what it does. Change the impostor used by a block with a SphereImpostor, and see what it does.

CHEAT SHEET

Enable the physics engine (HTML part):

```
<script src="lib/OIMO.js"></script>
```

Enable the physics engine (JS part):

```
scene.enablePhysics(new BABYLON.Vector3(0, -9.5, 0), new
BABYLON.OimoJSPlugin());
```

Set an impostor:

```
var body = mesh.setPhysicsState(BABYLON.PhysicsEngine.BoxImpostor, {mass:0,
restitution : 0.5, friction:0.5});
```

Apply an impulse:

```
mesh.applyImpulse(force, position);
```

force: BABYLON.Vector3 ⇨ the force of the impulse

position: BABYLON.Vector3 ⇨ the impulse position

CHAPTER 11 - COLLISIONS AND ACTIONS

Currently, we have a pretty slick game: the player can move, turn around, it can even fall off the ground. But you surely noticed that moving into the spikes or in the key does nothing.

In this chapter, we will use two different concepts to monitor collisions between the player and each element of the world. First, we will use the standard collision engine by checking collisions between the player mesh and each game object. Then, we will discover the action system of Babylon.js which describes an action to be launched when a condition is fulfilled.

Collision engine

Babylon.js provides a built-in collision system that can be used to detect if two meshes are colliding with each other. It consists of several methods on the **AbstractMesh** class:

- intersectsMesh
- intersectsPoint
- intersectsRay

How does it work?

For each mesh in the scene, Babylon.js automatically creates a bounding volume. Actually, there are two bounding volumes: a bounding box, and a bounding sphere.

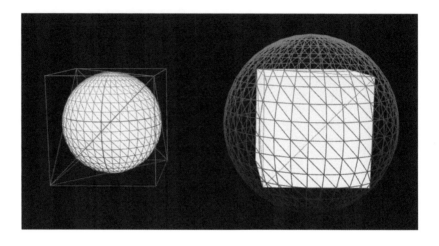

Figure 39 - Bounding sphere and bounding box for two meshes

On the image above, the mesh is in white. For each mesh, the bounding sphere is in blue, and the bounding box is in orange.

To avoid intensive calculations to have pixel perfect collisions, Babylon.js tests intersections between bounding volumes of the two colliding mesh.

Intersection with another mesh

The method intersectsMesh takes two parameters: the other mesh to test the intersection with, and a boolean. This boolean is the precision of the intersection. If it is set to 'false', the system will only do an AABB (Axis-Aligned Bounding Box) collision check (the fastest and simplest one). If it is set to true, the system will do an OBB (Oriented Bounding Box) collision check. This kind of collision detection is more costly, but it can be useful if your mesh is rotated (as AABB collision doesn't check the object orientation at all).

The corresponding code is just below:

```
if (box.intersectsMesh(otherMesh, true)) {
  // Collision ! Do something here.
}
```

Sometimes, as the collision engine uses meshes' bounding volumes, it can be useful to compute these volumes by using the method computeWorldMatrix.

```
box.computeWorldMatrix(true);
```

Intersection with a point

The parameter true forces the recalculation of these volumes. Without this parameter, bounding volumes will be updated only if needed. The method intersectsPoint can be used to check if a mesh collides with a given point (BABYLON.Vector3). It returns true if there is a collision, or false otherwise.

Intersection with a ray

A ray is a very simple thing can be defined by an origin point and a direction. In Babylon.js, it can be built like this:

```
var start = BABYLON.Vector3.Zero();
var direction = BABYLON.Vector3.Up();
var ray = new BABYLON.Ray(start, direction);
```

In this case, the ray will start at the world origin (0,0,0) and go towards the Y axis (0,1,0).

This ray can be used to check if a mesh is in the ray's path (or in others words: if the ray intersects this mesh). Like the two methods above, its use is very simple:

```
var pickInfo = box.intersects(ray, true);
```

The first parameter is the ray, and the second parameter indicates if the system should stop at the first collision found.

The result of this method is an instance of the class **BABYLON.PickingInfo**. This class presents these interesting parameters:

hit	True if the ray touched anything, false otherwise.
distance	The distance between the origin of the ray and the picked point.
pickedPoint	A **Vector3** representing the intersecting point of the mesh.
pickedMesh	The instance of the mesh that intersects with this ray.
bu bv	Coordinates texture of the picked points.

Be careful, the origin of the ray given in parameter must be set in the local world of the mesh.

Detect collisions between player and spikes

Let's set up a collision detector in our game. First, create a method that will run in the same time as the game render loop. We will be using the method **registerBeforeRender** of the game scene:

```
var _this = this;
this.scene.registerBeforeRender(function() {
```

```
_this.checkCollisions();
});
```

The method **checkCollisions** will first check if the player has been spiked, then if the player has finished the current level, and finally if he has taken a key:

```
Game.prototype.checkCollisions = function() {
  // If player spiked
  if (this.level.canKill(this.player)) {
    this.reset();
  }
  // If level finished
  else if (this.level.canGetApple(this.player)){
    this.nextLevel();
  }
  else {
    // If collide with key, remove the corresponding spike
    var key = this.level.canGetKey(this.player);
    if (key) {
      key.removeSpike();
    }
  }
};
```

Then, in the Level class, the method **canKill** will check if the player intersects with each **Spike** instance, and returns a boolean accordingly:

```
/**
 * Returns true if at least one spike object intersects with the player.
 * Otherwise returns false.
 * @param player
 */
Level.prototype.canKill = function(player) {
  var res = false;
  this.spikes.forEach(function(s) {
    // Intersection !
    if (s.sharpPart.intersectsMesh(player)) {
      res = true;
    }
  });
  return res;
};
```

If you run your game right now, the game should reset by moving the player on a spike. Of course, there is no death animation in this example (nor is there a game over screen), but it should not be very difficult to add one in the future.

Exercise

Implement the method level.canGetApple(player) and level.canGetKey(player). In our current implementation, the Spike class, the Key class and the Apple class extends Mesh for position easing, but have no geometry. The method mesh.getChildren() could be used to returns the list of children of each instance.

Using actions to check collisions

Babylon.js has a built-in action system that can add a specific behaviour to a mesh when a condition is fulfilled. The behaviour is called an action, which is launched when a trigger is fired. This action can also be configured with a condition to create a very powerful conditional system.

For example, you can launch the action '*update the mesh material color*' when the trigger '*a player clicks on a mesh*' is fired. The trigger can only be fired if the condition '*the player has more than one life*' is fulfilled. All this in less than 10 lines of code ☺

How to use it

First, you have to create an instance of the class BABYLON.ActionManager and link it to your mesh.

```
mesh.actionManager = new BABYLON.ActionManager(scene);
```

The only parameter to give to the ActionManager is the game scene, which will be used to check for trigger (in the render loop... as we did for collisions in the previous chapter!).

Actions

There are several kind of actions available, as the table below describes it:

SetValueAction	Set the given value to the specified target property.
IncrementValueAction	Add the given number to the given property.
PlaySoundAction	Play the given sound.
StopSoundAction	Stop the given sound.
SetParentAction	Update the parent node of the given target.
SetStateAction	Update the attribute 'state' on the target with the specified value.
InterpolateValueAction	Create an animation from the current value to the given value.
PlayAnimationAction	Launch an animation on a given target.
StopAnimationAction	Stop all animations on the given target.
SwitchBooleanAction	Toggle the value of the specified property.
CombineAction	Combine an array of action to be executed for the same trigger.
DoNothingAction	Does nothing at all, but can be combined with others.
ExecuteCodeAction	Run the given function when the trigger is fired.

Triggers

To create a new action, you have to instantiate it with a trigger. There are different kind of triggers as described in the table below. The trigger is fired when the corresponding user action is done:

OnPickTrigger	Click (mouse down) on the target mesh.
OnPickUpTrigger	Click (mouse up) on the target mesh.
OnLeftPickTrigger	Left click on the mesh.
OnRightPickTrigger	Right click on the mesh.
OnCenterPickTrigger	Center click on the mesh.
OnPointerOverTrigger	The mouse is over the target mesh. Raised only once.
OnPointerOutTrigger	The mouse is no more over the target mesh. Raised only once.
OnKeyDownTrigger	A key has been pressed (keydown).
OnKeyUpTrigger	A key has been released (keyup).
OnIntersectionEnterTrigger	The target mesh intersects with another mesh. Raised just once.
OnIntersectionExitTrigger	The target mesh no longer intersects with another mesh. Raised just once.
OnEveryFrameTrigger	Raised every frame.
NothingTrigger	No trigger is needed (used to chain actions).

For example, let's say you want to set the value of the diffuse color of a mesh to black by clicking on it (to select it):

```
var action = new
BABYLON.SetValueAction(BABYLON.ActionManager.OnPickTrigger, mesh.material,
"diffuseColor", BABYLON.Color3.Green());
mesh.actionManager.registerAction(action);
```

And that's it! Simple, right?

Some triggers require parameters: for example, OnIntersectionEnterTrigger needs to have a reference to the other mesh the target mesh will collide with.

In this case, the first parameter to give to the action is an object with two attributes: **trigger** (which is the kind of trigger that will be used), and **parameter** (the trigger parameter).

Below is the same behavior as above but the color is now changed with an intersection with another mesh called mesh2:

```
var trigger = {trigger:BABYLON.ActionManager.OnIntersectionEnterTrigger,
parameter: mesh2};
var action = new BABYLON.SetValueAction(trigger, mesh.material, "diffuseColor",
BABYLON.Color3.Green());
mesh.actionManager.registerAction(action);
```

Conditions

Finally, the trigger is raised when the action condition is fulfilled. 3 different kind of conditions exists:

ValueCondition	True when the given property is equal/greater than a specific value.
PredicateCondition	Use the function given in parameter to check if the condition is true.
StateCondition	Check the attribute state of the target and compare it with the given value.

Personally, I would use an ExecuteCodeAction to use my own code instead of having to use a Condition, but it's a good thing to be aware of their existence.

Look at the code below:

```
sphere.actionManager = new BABYLON.ActionManager(scene);
var action = new
BABYLON.IncrementValueAction(BABYLON.ActionManager.OnPickTrigger, sphere,
"scaling.x",1,
  new BABYLON.ValueCondition(sphere.actionManager, sphere, "scaling.x", 3,
BABYLON.ValueCondition.IsLesser)
);
sphere.actionManager.registerAction(action);
```

Can you guess its behaviour? The answer is just below ☺

An **IncrementValueAction** is created, and is fired on a pick action. When the user clicks on the sphere, the trigger will be raised, and the property **scaling.x** will be incremented by 1. Finally, this action will be done only if the property **scaling.x** of the sphere is lesser than 3.

Using actions to check collisions

As you surely know, we will use the trigger **OnIntersectionEnterTrigger** to check for collisions between our player and game objects.
Here is the code for the key:

```
// First things first: action manager creation
key.actionManager = new BABYLON.ActionManager(this.getScene());
var _this = this;
// Create a trigger "on intersection with the player"
var trigger = {trigger:BABYLON.ActionManager.OnIntersectionEnterTrigger,
parameter: _this.game.player};
// If the trigger is raised, execute some code
var removeSpikeAction = new BABYLON.ExecuteCodeAction(trigger, function() {
  _this.setEnabled(false);
  _this.spike.setEnabled(false);
});// Finally register the action
key.actionManager.registerAction(removeSpikeAction);
```

Exercise

Try to add actions for the Spike object, and for the Apple class. Each time, an **ExecuteCodeAction** should be used to call these two methods from the Game class: **game.nextLevel()**, or **game.reset()**.

CHEAT SHEET

Check intersection with another mesh:

```
if (box.intersectsMesh(otherMesh, true)) {
  // Collision ! Do something here.
}
```

Intersection between a ray and a mesh:

```
var start = BABYLON.Vector3.Zero();
var direction = BABYLON.Vector3.Up();
var ray = new BABYLON.Ray(start, direction);
var pickInfo = box.intersects(ray, true);
```

Create an Action Manager:

```
mesh.actionManager = new BABYLON.ActionManager(scene);
```

Register an action:

```
mesh.actionManager.registerAction(action);
```

CHAPTER 12 - SKELETONS AND BONES SYSTEM

A bone system is a hierarchical linkage of bones that can be used to animate 3D objects. They are useful especially if you want to animate a character or any model with a continuous mesh. In this chapter, we will talk about skeletons (the name for a bones system) and see how they can be exported from 3DSMax to Babylon.js, to be used in a game.

Skeletons

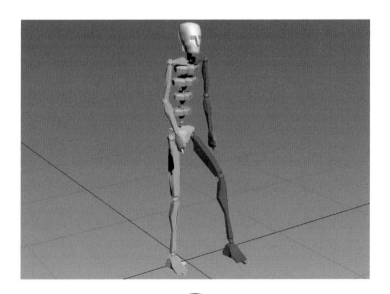

The image above shows a skeleton in 3DSMax. As you can see, this skeleton is not attached to any mesh (so it's completely useless), but you notice that each bone is a mesh that can be rendered in 3DSMax. However, if you export your skeleton as is in Babylon.js, you won't see anything... yet all meshes are here!

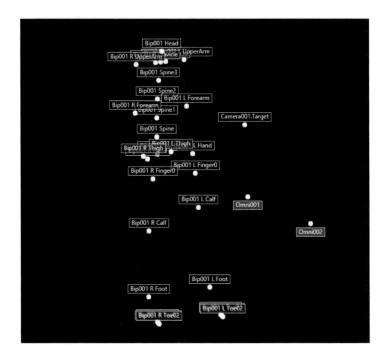

In practice, each bone will be attached to a mesh and will influence a specific number of vertices of the mesh. When the bone rotates, moves or is scaled, each vertex will react accordingly to the bone transformation.

In 3DSMax, a single vertex can be influenced by up to 20 bones (default value). Babylon.js supports skeletal animation with a maximum of 4 bones' influences per vertex. Before exporting your skeleton, you will have to update this value from 20 to at least 4, or your mesh will act strangely (update this value in the Skin modifier – Advanced Parameters)

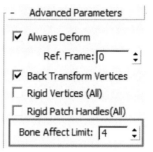

A skeleton and its animations are exported like any other meshes with the Max2Babylon plugin.

Load a skeleton in Babylon.js

Actually, all methods for loading a Babylon file will also load existing skeletons. We just have to use it ☺

ImportMesh function

Do you remember the ImportMesh function?

```
BABYLON.SceneLoader.ImportMesh(meshName, folderName, fileName, scene,
onSuccess, onProgress, onError);
```

The onSuccess function takes as last parameter an array containing all skeletons loaded by the engine. If your model has only one skeleton, you can do something like this in order to run its animation:

```
scene.beginAnimation(skeletons[0], 0, 120, 1.0, true);
```

It's exactly the same method as seen in CHAPTER 8 – Animations. Difficult, don't you think? ☺

Assets manager

When you create a new task for your assets manager, you can define the method onSuccess on a MeshTask and retrieve the loaded skeletons (as we did for loadedMeshes if you remember well):

```
var task = loader.addMeshTask(…);
task.onSuccess = function(t) {
    var skeletons = t.loadedSkeletons;
    scene.beginAnimation(skeletons[0], 0, 120, 1.0, true);
};
```

Loading a player in the game

In our game, we will use a custom character model that has been rigged and animated with Mixamo (https://www.mixamo.com), a website that automatically (and magically!) animates the model you upload on their platform.

Here is what our badass ninja looks like. Let's export it right away (just call it player.babylon) in our assets folder. Don't forget to copy all textures into the same folder.

First, we have to update the Game class, as it is responsible for loading assets.

```
var animsPlayer = [];
animsPlayer['walk'] = {from:0, to:30, speed:2, loop:false};
var toLoad = [
  ...,
  {
    name:"player",
    folder:"assets/player/",
    filename:"player.babylon",
    anims : animsPlayer
  }
];
```

Finally, update the onSuccess method to keep an eye on skeletons:

```
task.onSuccess = function(t) {
  ...
  // Save it in the asset array
```

```
_this.assets[t.name] = {meshes:t.loadedMeshes, anims:tl.anims, skeletons:
t.loadedSkeletons};
};
```

The next part will be done in the Player class. In its constructor, add some lines to scale down our player (he's BIG) and to retrieve our skeletons:

```
var meshes = game.assets['player'].meshes;
var skeletons = game.assets['player'].skeletons;
var walk = game.assets['player'].anims['walk'];
var _this = this;
meshes.forEach(function(m) {
  m.parent = _this;
  m.isVisible = true;
  m.scaling = new BABYLON.Vector3(0.05,0.05,0.05);
  m.position = BABYLON.Vector3.Zero();
  m.position.y -= 0.75/2;
});
this.skeletons = skeletons;
this.fromFrame = walk.from;
this.toFrame = walk.to;
```

In our character mesh, there are two skeletons: one for the body and one for both hands. Don't ask me why, it's the magic of Mixamo: it just works ☺

In the Player move function, add something to stop all animations if our player is not impacted by any physics force:

```
Player.prototype.move = function() {
  ...
  if (this.body.body.sleeping) {
    this._animateSkeletons();
  } else {
    this.getScene().stopAnimation(this);
  }
};
```

The method _animateSkeleton is as follows:

```
/**
 * Animate the player skeletons.
 * @private
 */
Player.prototype._animateSkeletons = function() {
  for (var i=0; i<this.skeletons.length; i++) {
    this.getScene().beginAnimation(this.skeletons[i], this.fromFrame, this.toFrame,
true);
  }
};
```

And that's it!

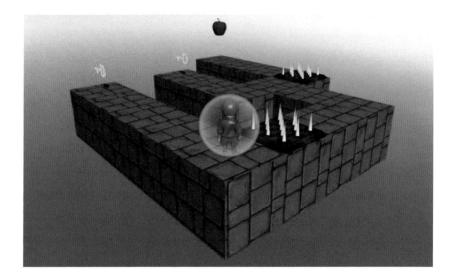

CHAPTER 13 - EYE CANDIES

Our game is almost done ☺. This chapter will show you how to create and instantiate particles systems to add some magic to your games. Finally, we will see how to apply a custom shader on a mesh to make it shiny and fabulous!

Particles, or how to simulate the real world

Particles are small sprites used to simulate interesting 3D effects that are otherwise very difficult to reproduce: for example natural phenomena (like fire, snow or rain), chemical reactions, and so on. Sprites are less costly than 3D models and thus can be emitted in a large number.

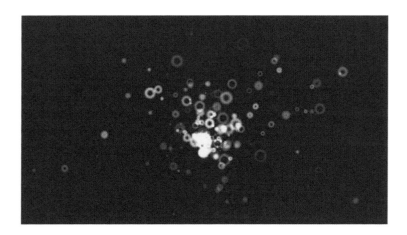

Particles can be generated with a specific object called a ParticleSystem. This object will take care of creating new particles and recycling old ones.

```
var particleSystem = new BABYLON.ParticleSystem("particles", 2000, scene);
```

The constructor takes 3 parameters:
- The system name
- The max number of particles
- The Babylon scene

The system can then be heavily configured. Here is the list of important parameters. An exhaustive list can be found in the documentation here: http://doc.babylonjs.com/tutorials/particles

particleTexture	A BABYLON.Texture representing the aspect of each particle
emitter	Can be a 3D object or a position. Represents the position of each particle when emitted.
minEmitBox maxEmitBox	Vector3 representing the min and max point where particles are emitted.
color1 color2 colorDead	BABYLON.Color4 representing particles' colors.
minSize maxSize	Particle sizes will be in this range
minLifeTime maxLifeTime	Each particle's life time will be a random number in this range.
emitRate	The system emission rate.
direction1 direction2	Each particle will be given a direction randomly in this range.

After being configured, a system can be launched with the method start (and stopped with the method stop of course):

```
particleSystem.start();
particleSystem.stop();
```

The magic key

In our game, each key will have a particle system attached to it, to add a little bit of magic (or faery dust ☺)

The source code won't be displayed entirely here as it is really simple. It's all about configuration:

```
Key.prototype.initParticles = function() {
  var particleSystem = new BABYLON.ParticleSystem("particles", 2000,
this.getScene());

  //Texture of each particle
  particleSystem.particleTexture = new BABYLON.Texture("assets/flare.png",
this.getScene());

  // Where the particles come from
  particleSystem.emitter = this.getChildren()[0];
  particleSystem.minEmitBox = new BABYLON.Vector3(0, -1, -1);
  particleSystem.maxEmitBox = new BABYLON.Vector3(0, 3, 1);
  //... some more configuration...
  return particleSystem;
```

```
};
```

Shaders and custom effects

What is a shader?

A shader is a (usually) small computer program coded for the GPU unit (your graphic card) that determines how 3D surface properties of objects are rendered, and how light interacts with this object.

There are two kinds of shaders:

- **fragment shaders** (or pixel shaders), that operates on a per pixel basis and take care of stuff like colors and lighting.

- **vertex shaders**, that are more oriented on the geometry of the object (or the scene).

Several kind of variables can be given to these program, like the camera's point of view, a specific color, and so on (but we will see that later).

These shaders are written in GLSL (Graphics Library Shader Language), a programming language that looks like C but has its particular specification (defined on the official OpenGL webpage here https://www.opengl.org/documentation/glsl/).

In Babylon.js, there are two ways of defining a shader: directly in the HTML file, or in external files.

In your HTML page, define your two shaders (or more if you like) like this:

```
<script type="application/vertexShader" id="vertexShaderCode">
    //...
</script>
<script type="application/fragmentShader" id="fragmentShaderCode">
```

```
   //...
</script>
```

In my opinion, the best way is to define external files in a specific folder called **shaders** (I love originality).

Create Your Own Shader - CYOS

CYOS is a website built over Babylon.js dedicated to give you the best place to create and see your shader immediately.

It is composed of two code editors (one for the vertex shader, and one for the fragment shader), and a Babylon.js view to see your shader automatically. There are few predefined shaders: in the above image, the displayed shader is called Spherical Environment mapping. Let's take a look at it for a moment.

Here is the vertex shader:

```
precision highp float;

// Attributes
attribute vec3 position;
attribute vec3 normal;
```

```
attribute vec2 uv;

// Uniforms
uniform mat4 worldViewProjection;

// Varying
varying vec4 vPosition;
varying vec3 vNormal;

void main() {

  vec4 p = vec4( position, 1. );

  vPosition = p;
  vNormal = normal;

  gl_Position = worldViewProjection * p;

}
```

You can already see it is divided into 4 distinct blocks:

- Attributes
- Uniforms
- Varying
- A main() function.

Attributes are variables used to communicate from "outside" the shader, which are defined only in the vertex shader.

Uniforms are, like attributes, variables used to communicate from "outside" the shader (read-only access). Unlike attributes, these data are provided globally for all vertices.

Varying variables are interfaces between the vertex shader and the fragment shader.

The main function is executed by the GPU and must returns a variable gl_Position for the vertex shader, and gl_FragColor for the fragment shader.

In this vertex shader, 3 attributes are used: position, normal and uv. Babylon.js uses these attribute names to bind each one to the corresponding vertex buffer of the mesh the shader will be applied on. It's almost the same for uniforms, as they are custom values given to the shader.

The fragment shader is almost similar:

```
precision highp float;

uniform mat4 worldView;

varying vec4 vPosition;
varying vec3 vNormal;

uniform sampler2D refSampler;

void main(void) {

    vec3 e = normalize( vec3( worldView * vPosition ) );
    vec3 n = normalize( worldView * vec4(vNormal, 0.0) ).xyz;

    vec3 r = reflect( e, n );
    float m = 2. * sqrt(
        pow( r.x, 2. ) +
        pow( r.y, 2. ) +
        pow( r.z + 1., 2. )
    );
    vec2 vN = r.xy / m + .5;

    vec3 base = texture2D( refSampler, vN).rgb;

    gl_FragColor = vec4( base, 1. );
}
```

You can see there are no attributes here, as they can only be used in the vertex shader.

Once you have your shader ready to go (thanks to CYOS), you can start adding it to your game.

Using a custom shader

In the game, create a folder shaders and create two files: shiny.vertex.fx and shiny.fragment.fx. The first one will contain the vertex shader and the second one is the fragment shader.

A shader is used with the class BABYLON.ShaderMaterial:

```
var shaderMat = new BABYLON.ShaderMaterial(name, scene, shaderPathName, options);
```

Parameters name and scene should be familiar to you. shaderPathName can have two different values:

    - If you decided to save your shader directly in the HTML page, it should be an object with two parameters vertexElement and fragmentElement. Values are the ID of <script> tag in your HTML file:

```
{
    vertexElement: "vertexShaderCode",
    fragmentElement: "fragmentShaderCode"
}
```

    - If you decided to save your shader in external files, it should be the file name given to the shader files (in our case 'shiny'). The system will concatenate your name with the global variable BABYLON.Engine.ShadersRepository and '.vertex.fx' and '.fragment.fx'. Don't forget to set this variable to suit your project. Here is the default value:

```
BABYLON.Engine.ShadersRepository = "Babylon/Shaders/";
```

The last parameter options is an object containing several attributes:
    - needAlphaBlending (default to false)
    - needAlphaTesting (default to false)

- samplers (default to [])
- defaultsattributes (default to ["position", "normal", "uv"])
- uniforms (default to ["worldViewProjection"]).

You are totally right, attributes and uniforms are exactly the same as in our shader files! We will use this parameter to define which variable is an attribute or a uniform.

In our game (class Key), the method createShader is used to assign the shiny shader to the key instance.

```
Key.prototype.createShader = function(){
  // Shader creation
  var shader = new BABYLON.ShaderMaterial("shinny", this.game.scene, "shinny", {
    uniforms: ["worldView", "worldViewProjection"]
  });
  // Texture creation
  var refTexture = new BABYLON.Texture("assets/hdri/hdri.jpg", this.game.scene);
  refTexture.wrapU = BABYLON.Texture.CLAMP_ADDRESSMODE;
  refTexture.wrapV = BABYLON.Texture.CLAMP_ADDRESSMODE;
  // Link the texture to the shader
  shader.setTexture("refSampler", refTexture);
  // And you're done!
  return shader;
};
```

The shader material creation is done in the first line of the method: its name is shiny (first parameter), and the file name to retrieve are called shiny (third parameter). In the Game class, this line is present:

```
BABYLON.Engine.ShadersRepository = "shaders/";
```

This means the system will look for all shaders in a folder called shaders. Exactly what we want!

The last parameter of our ShaderMaterial is an object containing only one attribute:

```
{ uniforms: ["worldView", "worldViewProjection"]}
```

Babylon.js provides 6 default uniforms that are automatically filled when a new ShaderMaterial is created:

- view: the scene view matrix
- projection: the scene projection matrix
- viewProjection: the scene transform matrix
- world: the mesh world matrix
- worldView: the mesh world matrix multiplied by the scene view matrix
- worldViewProjection: the mesh world matrix multiplied by the scene transform matrix.

You are already aware of the object world matrix (representing the object position, scaling and rotation). The scene view matrix represents the camera position and the camera target. The projection matrix represents data to transform the 3D into the 2D world (screen), like the viewport size, the field of view, and so on.

By filling the option object with worldView and worldViewProjection, we are just telling Babylon.js "Here is my shader, and I need these two variables please".

The last thing our shader needs is a reflection texture (called refSampler). Once the texture has been created, the method setTexture is used on the shader material. You can also use these methods:

- setFloat
- setFloats
- setColor3
- setColor4
- setVector2
- setVector3
- setMatrix
- setTexture

The last thing to do: link our material to our mesh!

```
key.material = this.createShader();
```

Actually, you have been using shaders from the beginning without even knowing it ☺ In Babylon, all materials are internally represented by shaders, and it's done automatically!

CHAPTER 14 - IMPROVING PERFORMANCE

When you're dealing with a large number of objects, performance can become an issue. Generally speaking, you want the highest framerate possible (close to the mighty 60 FPS). This chapter offers tips and suggestions to improve the global performance and the framerate of your game/application running on Babylon.js. In this section, we will see:

      - How to merge meshes in order to reduce the number of draw calls

      - What are octrees and how using them improves performance

      - How to set several levels of detail for a specific object.

Merging multiple meshes

Let's try a simple performance experiment using the Babylon.js playground: I want to display as many boxes as possible while keeping a constant 60 FPS.

The code itself is not very complicated:

```
/**
 * Returns a number between min and max.
 */
var randomInt = function (min, max) {
  var random = Math.random();
```

```
  return ((random * (max - min)) + min);
};

var createScene = function () {

  // Scene
  var scene = new BABYLON.Scene(engine);

  // Camera
  var camera = new BABYLON.ArcRotateCamera("camera1", 0, Math.PI/3, 250,
  BABYLON.Vector3.Zero(), scene);
  camera.attachControl(canvas);

  // Light
  var light = new BABYLON.HemisphericLight("light1", new BABYLON.Vector3(0, 1,
  0), scene);

  var NB_BOXES = 1000;
  var boxes = [];

  // Create each box
  for (var i = 0; i < NB_BOXES; i++) {
    var box = BABYLON.Mesh.CreateBox("box" + i, randomInt(2, 6), scene);
    box.position = new BABYLON.Vector3(
    randomInt(-200, 200),
    randomInt(-200, 200),
    randomInt(-200, 200)
    );
    boxes.push(box);
  }

  // Make the camera rotate automatically
  scene.registerBeforeRender(function () {
    camera.alpha += 0.01;
  });

  return scene;
};
```

The result is a lot a boxes rendered at... 24 FPS.

A solution to improve this behaviour is to merge all boxes into a big mesh, using the method BABYLON.Mesh.MergeMeshes:

```
var mergedMesh = BABYLON.Mesh.MergeMeshes(boxes, true, true);
```

This method takes 4 parameters:

- An array of BABYLON.Mesh representing the objects to merge

- A boolean disposeSource: set it to true to delete old objects after the merge.

- A boolean allow32BitsIndice: set it to true if your result mesh can have more than 65536 vertices (but it might not work on some devices)

- A class name representing a Mesh sub-class (GameObject for example – see chapter CHAPTER 4 - Working with classes)

With this line, our set of cubes is rendered at 60 FPS. And we can even set the number of cubes to 20000, while the demo is still rendered at 60 FPS!

Of course, it has some limitations. As the merged mesh is only one object, it can have only one material. Similarly, it won't be possible to move each box independently: the merged object will act as a single big shape.

Octrees

Wikipedia has a good definition of an octree: "An octree is a tree data structure in which each internal node has exactly eight children." (https://en.wikipedia.org/wiki/Octree)

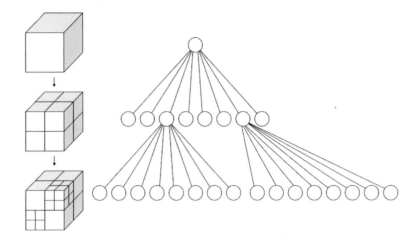

As we can see in the image above (credits to Wikipedia), the 3D world will be separated into 8 blocks, and each block will then be separated into 8 blocks, and so on, until all 3D objects are in a given block of the octree.

Creating an octree for your scene can help the system to quickly select meshes that need to be rendered (if whether the object is in front of the camera or not), or help compute intersections quickly.

Optimize mesh selection

In one line of code, you can create an octree: the system will use it automatically when needed:

```
var octree = scene.createOrUpdateSelectionOctree();
```

Be careful, an octree is static. That means you will need to recompute it (with the same line of code) each time you add a mesh in your scene, or each time a mesh moves in your scene.

Optimize mesh picking

When a mesh is too complex (more than 10k vertices for example), you can optimize picking and intersections operations with 2 steps. First, you have to subdivide the mesh into several sub-meshes:

```
mesh.subdivide(10) ;
```

The parameter represents the number of sub-meshes you need. Then, just call the octree creation like this:

```
mesh.createOrUpdateSubmeshesOctree();
```

Level Of Detail (LOD)

The level of detail (or LOD) of an object is a way to define its complexity according to the distance between the active camera and this object. This technique increases performance by reducing the number of triangles to display when the user is too far away to notice it.
In Babylon.js, the level of detail of a mesh is applied to the object geometry and/or to its material/texture.

There are two distinct processes to set a level of detail to an object. The first one is a simplification of the mesh (the LOD is automatically created by the system), and the second one needs you to specify another mesh that will be displayed instead.

Mesh auto simplification

The decimation process is fairly easy to use: a BABYLON.Mesh instance has a method called simplify:

```
Mesh.prototype.simplify = function (settings, parallelProcessing,
simplificationType, successCallback)
```

This function takes 4 parameters:

- settings is an array of BABYLON.SimplificationSettings (which is defined below)

- parallelProcessing is a boolean indicating if all simplifications (defined in the settings array) should be done asynchronously.

- simplificationType is the kind of simplification done to the mesh (only one type for the moment: BABYLON.SimplificationType.QUADRATIC)

- successCallback is a function called when the simplification is finished.

An instance of a BABYLON.SimplificationSettings is composed of 3 parameters:

- quality is a number between 0 and 1 representing the percentage of the decimation (for example, a quality set to 0.6 will simplify the mesh by keeping 60% of its faces).

- distance is a number indicating the distance between the camera and the mesh to enable the simplification.

- optimizeMesh is a boolean indicating if the mesh should be optimized beforehand.

Let's try to use simplification on a simple sphere:

```
// sphere creation
var sphere = BABYLON.Mesh.CreateSphere("sphere", 60, 9, scene);

// simplification settings
var s1 = new BABYLON.SimplificationSettings(0.5, 20, true); // at distance 20, only
50% of faces will be kept
var s2 = new BABYLON.SimplificationSettings(0.1, 40, true); // at distance 40, only
10% of faces will be kept

// decimation
sphere.simplify([s1, s2], true, BABYLON.SimplificationType.QUADRATIC);
```

Here are the results:

Settings	Solid	Wireframe
No simplificatio n active indices: 46128		
quality: 50% distance: 20 active indices: 23064		
quality: 10% distance: 40 active indices: 4608		

As you can see, the number of active indices of the sphere decreases with the decimation process: the whole geometry is updated, but the general shape is kept.

Try to use this simplification process with complex meshes with a high number of faces: there is no sense using it on simple objects, as a removed face will probably create a hole.

Adding a LOD level

Manually adding a LOD level to a mesh is approximately the same system: you define a new mesh (with a new material if needed) that will be displayed when the active camera is at a certain distance of this object.

This way of adding a LOD level uses the method addLODLevel for a BABYLON.Mesh:

```
mesh.addLODLevel(15, meshLOD1);
mesh.addLODLevel(30, meshLOD2);
```

This method takes 2 parameters:

- The distance beyond which the LOD mesh will be displayed
- The LOD mesh to display after the specified distance

In the case above, if the distance between mesh and the player is more than 15, meshLOD1 will be displayed. If the distance is more than 30, meshLOD2 will be displayed.

By using null as second parameter, the original mesh will not be rendered.

Keep in mind that all objects specified as LOD meshes are linked to the original mesh and thus cannot be rendered directly.

If you want to remove a LOD level, just use the method removeLODLevel ☺

```
mesh.removeLODLevel(meshLOD1);
```

Using instances and clones

If you have several identical meshes, they can easily be replaced by clones or instances (as explained in Chapter Clones and instances):

- All clones share the same geometry object, and thus optimize all meshes in memory.
- All instances share the same geometry object and the same material.

Of course, instances are your best choice if you want to represent a lot of objects having exactly the same geometry and material.

Optimize your textures

As said in the chapter Small talk about draw calls, each different image will represent a new draw call. There are two characteristics you can reduce in order to improve the frame computation, and thus improve the global FPS counter of your game:

- The number of textures
- The texture resolution

The image resolution is the number of bits used to store this image. It is defined by this simple calculation:

$$width * height * 8\ bits * channel\_number$$

Each channel of the image (red, blue, green, alpha) is stored on 8 bits: for a JPEG (3 channels because no alpha), this calculation is then:

$$width * height * 24\ bits$$

The image's width and height has a direct impact on the resolution, and thus on the duration of the frame computation.

The number of textures plays a direct role as well: if you can pack multiple images into a single big texture, the performance will be better. This technique is always used in video games: a 3D artist can create a texture atlas by unwrapping the 3D model and link each mesh to different texture coordinates. Here is the unwrap used for my ninja:

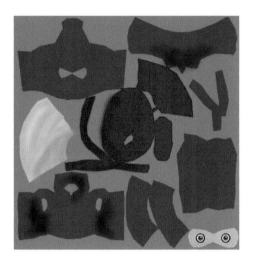

Going further

If you want to go further about Babylon.js architecture and how things works under the hood, I strongly recommend the book WebGL Insights, written by a lot of WebGL experts (and edited by Patrick Cozzi). David Catuhe is one of them, and a whole chapter is dedicated to Babylon.js. He can be found on Amazon for a price range from $50-$60.

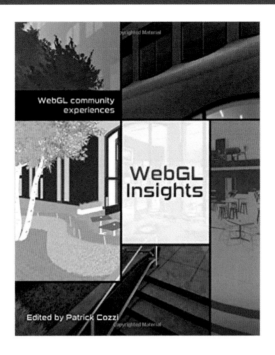

CONCLUSION

In this book about Babylon.js, we talk about a lot of things. First, we saw how to get started with the framework by creating a 3D cube in your browser. This was a first step to make you understand how easy it is to deal with Babylon.js: indeed, with only a few lines of code you were able to create this small application and make it running.

Then, we described several concepts commonly used in a standard game: materials, textures, external 3D models, collisions, physics... With all this knowledge, I hope you are now able to create your own Babylon.js game.

A question that is commonly answered on Babylon.js forum is: "Ok, I created my WebGL game. Can I wrap it into an iOS/Android/Windows Phone application in order to make some money from it?"

Indeed you can! The easiest way is to create a Windows application. Since the launch of Windows 8 (and now with Windows 10), you can easily create HTML5 applications for sell in the Windows Store. And guess what? Babylon.js is supported out of the box☺. That means your awesome WebGL game can automatically be deployed on the Windows Store.

It's not that easy for iOS and Android, but you can try to use Cocoon.js, a deployment platform created by Ludei. Cocoon.js acts as an application wrapper creating a web view to run your game. The mode 'Canvas+' recently created is very powerful for full WebGL games (Only a HTML canvas is created: no DOM, no XML is supported).

There are many features of Babylon.js I didn't have the opportunity to talk about, like procedural textures, lens flares, special visual effects, post-process (and more), but I think you have everything you need to understand it by yourself. Good luck to you, and if you come by the official forum, don't hesitate to come and say hello ☺

ACKNOWLEDGMENT

There are many people I would like to thank. First of all, my friend and colleague Jean-Baptiste, who made an awesome job at creating a cover for this book. I also would like to thank all the other people from my office for their advices and their encouragements (big up Anthony, Zacaria, François!)

I also would like to thank David Catuhe (also known as Deltakosh), Michel Rousseau and David Rousset (also known as Davrous) for creating the great library Babylon.js. David took some of his time to write the preface of this book, and I really appreciate that.

Thank you to all the forum member I talk to almost every day: Raanan (Programming guru), gryff (Blender-master!), Wingnut (XML lover and tutorial maker), dad72 (castor-engine FTW), JC-Palmer (Blender-master as well), Jerome (All you need is tubes!) and more generally to all contributors of this awesome engine.

Finally, thank you to my wife and my son, who gave me the motivation and the support I needed.

23654381R10119

Printed in Great Britain
by Amazon